The American Jesus?

The American Jesus?

DOUGLAS JOHNSON

WIPF & STOCK · Eugene, Oregon

THE AMERICAN JESUS?

Copyright © 2020 Douglas Johnson. All rights reserved. Except for brief quotations in critical publications or reviews, no part of this book may be reproduced in any manner without prior written permission from the publisher. Write: Permissions, Wipf and Stock Publishers, 199 W. 8th Ave., Suite 3, Eugene, OR 97401.

Wipf & Stock
An Imprint of Wipf and Stock Publishers
199 W. 8th Ave., Suite 3
Eugene, OR 97401

www.wipfandstock.com

PAPERBACK ISBN: 978-1-7252-5885-3
HARDCOVER ISBN: 978-1-7252-5886-0
EBOOK ISBN: 978-1-7252-5887-7

Manufactured in the U.S.A.   07/09/20

Biblical quotations are taken from the Revised Standard Version, 2nd edition, copyright © 1971 by the Division of Christian Education of the National Council of the Churches of Christ in the United States of America. Used by permission. All rights reserved.

Contents

Preface | vii

Introduction: Faith, Hope, and Love | 1
1. Faith (1) | 20
2. Faith (2) | 41
3. Hope | 62
4. Love | 82
Afterthoughts/Conclusions | 98

Bibliography | 109

Preface

SOME PERSONAL THOUGHTS: FOR many years, certainly by the time of my doctoral dissertation in 1969, one question has continually bothered me: the relation of my faith to my culture. To put the matter somewhat crudely: I want to be a good Christian. I also want to be a good American. Are they the same thing? Are they basically opposed, at odds with one another? Do they overlap? And if so, where, and to what extent?

I believe that many sincere persons have struggled with similar questions, and likely reached many differing answers. But there are also many holding on to both intentions, who may go on their merry way without being aware that they have a problem!

So this book is autobiographical, but it also intends to serve as a kind of guidebook for those who might be dealing with the same issue. I have not come to any earth-shaking conclusions for myself or for others. Yet I do hope that by giving both a historical and a theological treatment of the matter, I may be of some help in at least guiding others through the thicket of faith and culture.

An underlying assumption of this book is that faithful Christians throughout the ages have already been struggling with this issue, and some of them have come up with answers that, although not absolute, can be helpful to us in our own journey through this thicket. So in this journey, we may find, hopefully, a number of faithful believers who can be helpful as we look at our own assumptions and our own culture. Persons from other cultures may find much that is presented here applicable to their own, and helpful also to them.

Preface

This endeavor should not be and need not be an abstract enterprise. The issues are too existentially important for many of us. First, because many may have lost sight of what is at the heart of our faith. A review of the basics of that faith and how it has been understood and embraced by some of the great saints and thinkers who have gone before us might well reorient some of us who have lost sight of what is and has always been essential.

Second, it is crucial for Christians to realize that we are under increasing attack, often from some individuals and forces from within our own beloved culture. A review of the essential views and attitudes of that culture may enable us to see exactly what forces are arrayed against us. And even more, it may enable us to begin to see which attitudes of that culture have become part of our own thinking and are having important influences on the patterns of our faith and are affecting us unawares.

Third, and more positively: our becoming aware of the true bases of our Christian beliefs is particularly important in a world where believers and denominations within the body of Christ are divided and sometimes at each others' throats. It can help us to begin to overcome our narrow parochialism and work toward that unity for which Jesus himself prayed, when he prayed that his followers might all be one.

A thank you! to all of those who have given me good advice on this book.

Special thanks to Nathan Rhoads and Dr. James Aydellotte, whose careful reading and sound scholarship have been very helpful in this endeavor.

An even more enthusiastic thank you to my patient wife, Ann, whose support has been invaluable to me during this project.

Introduction
Faith, Hope, and Love

QUESTIONS CONCERNING AMERICAN CHRISTIANITY

Give, therefore to Caesar the things that are Caesar's and to God the things that are God's.

—MATT 22:21

TO SET THE STAGE for our journey, it might be helpful to take a trip to Plymouth, Massachusetts, the place where, as every American school child knows, the Pilgrims landed in 1620. There we will see a replica of the famous Mayflower, that sturdy little ship that crossed the Atlantic with its precious cargo of Pilgrims and other hardy and adventurous folk.

The stone near the water's edge is inscribed with the numbers 1620, which we are at liberty to believe were inscribed there at some later date.

There had been explorations and settlements before. But we can still see at Plymouth some historic images that can give us some insight into what the American experiment, especially in religion, is all about.

For one thing, most of these settlers were devout Christians, particularly influenced by the teachings of John Calvin, the great sixteenth-century reformer. But they differed from many other Calvinists in one regard. Unlike many Calvinists, they believed

The American Jesus?

in freedom of religion; that is, they believed in the separation of church and state, something thought very odd and even dangerous by many in that day. They had moved from England to the Netherlands, a place of more religious tolerance than in many other nations. Yet they decided to move on to the New World, to America. So we see that in the very beginning those who came here were by and large Europeans, and they were Christians of the Protestant faith. They had also come as those fearing persecution for that faith. They were seeking not only a new place, but a new start in a new world. It is also true, of course, that some of the passengers came for reasons other than religion.

If you go up to the top of the hill in Plymouth, you will see more. There stand two churches, almost side by side. They represent, not the early settlers, but the later developments of the area in culture and religion. One is a beautiful chapel. Its stained-glass windows are truly delightful. They portray, not biblical scenes, but events from the early New England leaders. The chapel proclaims itself as the church of the Pilgrims. This church is Unitarian, a denomination that finds its home more in the beliefs and hopes of the Enlightenment than in the theology of Calvinism, or, indeed, in traditional Christianity. As we shall see, this rational enlightened faith will to some extent replace traditional Christianity in much of New England and beyond.

Quite near to this Unitarian church there stands another, a Congregational church. There a sign proudly proclaims that, even if the other is the church of the Pilgrims, this is the church that has preserved the *faith* of those Pilgrims.

Whenever we deal with the issue of the Christian life, we find so many differing explanations of exactly what that is that it is hard to know where to start. Some concentrate on matters of correct belief and doctrine. Others stress individual commitment. For still others it is a matter of the heart. Perhaps all of these can give us some insight into what is central to the faith.

It is hard to find a better expression of this center than in the Apostle Paul's First Letter to the Corinthians, 13:13: "Faith, hope and love abide, but the greatest of these is love." Christians

Introduction

throughout the ages have wrestled with this simple phrase and have found in it riches that could be applied to their own personal struggles and to the culture in which they lived.

Another expression of this same idea is found in the fifth chapter of his Letter to the Romans:

> Therefore, being justified by faith, we have peace with God through our Lord Jesus Christ, through whom we have obtained access to this grace in which we stand; and we boast in our hope of sharing the glory of God. And not only that, but we also boast in our sufferings, knowing that suffering produces character and character produces hope, and hope does not disappoint us, because God's love has been shed abroad in our hearts through the Holy Spirit that has been given to us. (Rom 5:1–5)

An outstanding example of how central this view of the Christian life can be is found in a book written by no less than Augustine in the fifth century. He had been asked for a summary of the Christian faith. He responded with a handbook on this very faith,[1] a commentary on just this verse, which can still be relevant in our own struggles today.

Franklin D. Roosevelt was the longest-serving president that this nation has ever seen. While always surrounded by controversy, he did steer the United States through some of its darkest days, the Great Depression and World War II. He was the only U.S. president ever to be elected to four terms, something now forbidden by a constitutional amendment. Near the end of his life, when he took the oath of office for the fourth and last time, his hand was on his personal Bible. That book was opened to that same passage that was central to Paul and an inspiration to Augustine, ". . . faith, hope, and love, and the greatest of these is love."

It is hard to find anywhere in the world, or for that matter, anywhere in history, where the Christian community has found more success and prosperity than in America. In fact, many of the early American settlements were peopled by persons who were here precisely because of their faith, either escaping persecution,

---

1. Augustine, *Enchiridion*.

The American Jesus?

or striving to found a more perfect Christian society: Puritans in New England, Quakers and Presbyterians in Pennsylvania, Anglicans in most other colonies, Lutherans and Baptists here and there, with Roman Catholics in Maryland and elsewhere, and more. Eventually the Methodists would have phenomenal success in this land. Other home-grown denominations would spring up from time to time.

All of these would eventually find a home and fertile ground in which to grow under the cover of the First Amendment to the Constitution, where no religion is favored or supported over the others.

Yet with so many differing churches, there will necessarily be a variety of views about what is the correct understanding of the faith and what is the appropriate lifestyle of the believer. An interested observer may well be moved to ask which one of these is the real Christianity, or perhaps to wonder if any of them is. All of them can find something in the Bible or in church history to justify their beliefs and to question those of the others. We are left not only with the person's freedom to choose one's own religion, or none at all, but also with a kind of babel of voices, each proclaiming its own truth.

The miracle is that in the midst of all this, Christianity has grown and prospered in America in amazing ways, unheard of and unthinkable in other places and times. But the other side of this coin is that one is unclear on just what true Christianity might be.

THE CULTURE QUESTION

One facet of the problem of Christianity in America is that it is in America and thus cannot help but be influenced by that culture, or perhaps to a great extent be simply an expression of it. All of us are products of our culture, and that includes Christians as well as others. Clearly, Christianity has influenced various cultures over the years. But a parallel question is how much those cultures have influenced the faith itself. A Russian Orthodox will necessarily understand aspects of his or her life differently than a Southern Baptist or a medieval Roman Catholic.

Introduction

I recall a conversation that I had with a somewhat sophisticated couple. I casually mentioned that we are all influenced by our culture. "We are not!" they insisted. But in fact we all are! Family life, the media, our educational system, and our circle of friends all conspire to shape our view of life, of the world, of right and wrong, and even of ourselves and where we might "fit in." A belief that we are not so influenced can only increase the influence that our social conditioning has on us unawares, including, and perhaps especially, on our religious beliefs. To an extent, we might occasionally rise above this influence and be able to see beyond it, but these times are rare.

This issue has not gone unnoticed. Thinkers throughout the centuries have realized culture's influence on our beliefs. In his book *Protestant, Catholic, Jew*, Will Herberg suggests that in America there are no real Protestants, Catholics, or Jews, but only adherents to differing forms of the one religion, Americanism![2]

The classic work in the field is H. Richard Niebuhr's *Christ and Culture*, in which he suggests that there have been five differing approaches to the issue: Christ above culture, Christ of culture, Christ the transformer of culture, Christ in paradox with culture, and Christ against culture. All, apparently, have some claim to legitimacy.[3]

Clearly, my own approach differs from that of Niebuhr. While he lays out all of the basic possibilities of treating the issue, I concentrate on one approach, which I believe is well justified from both Scripture and Christian history. Perhaps this way of considering the matter overlaps or includes some of his alternatives.

THE ISSUE IN SCRIPTURE

This problem has been there for believers throughout history, beginning with the Bible. We might well begin by taking a look at

---

2. Herberg, *Protestant, Catholic, Jew*.

3 Niebuhr, *Christ and Culture*. See also Carlson, *Christ and Culture Revisited*. Also: Penner, ed., *Postmodern Turn*; Baker and Smith, *American Secularism*.

The American Jesus?

Abraham and the story of the near-sacrifice of Isaac in Genesis 22. Abraham heard the voice of God commanding him to sacrifice his son. And he intended to obey.

On its face, this story presents difficulties. But a closer examination may clarify it. It is clear that some of the pagan gods of that day did demand child sacrifice, and for Abraham this might have been a command of one such god. One of the pagan gods of that day was Elohim, a kind of general name for a god. The text in Genesis uses exactly that name for the god who demands this sacrifice. But when God said, "No! Do not sacrifice!," the name is Yahweh, the sacred name of the LORD given at the burning bush (Exodus 3). The tension here is between the true God and the deities of the surrounding culture.

Perhaps it is not too much to suggest that Abraham was not only the father of the Hebrew people, but also the prototype of all believers, and so of modern people. He is not some plaster saint, but a person who struggles to unite his surrounding culture with his faith in Yahweh. So, he may be very contemporary with us. We, in our world, modern as it may be, often find ourselves confused and at sea, wondering what we are to accept or reject in a surrounding world that is at the same time positive in its support of the human enterprise yet also destructive of some basic values. We have our own cultural gods calling to us. Like Abraham, we may have trouble sorting out what is from Yahweh and what is alien to the will of Yahweh.

The struggle was to continue throughout the history of this people. A short review of their history should make this plain.

When the people of Israel came into the promised land, that area was already occupied by other peoples with their own cultures and religions. The small scattered group of Israelites was hardly a match for the surrounding nations with their own gods and moralities. The choice was: either fight them or join them. Fighting often meant losing, with the possibility of the people being extinguished. Joining meant being absorbed into that other culture with its ways and its gods. Both ways were tried, and both could be disastrous.

Introduction

The people of Israel eventually came to rule the entire land, but corruption sometimes accompanied this victory, often in the form of adopting the ways of the nations already there. Prophets arose to protest the faithlessness of the land. They were usually ignored, and sometimes persecuted. Eventually the nation was divided, and the southern kingdom of Judah was sent into exile in Babylon, for about seventy years.

Allowed to return from exile, the people asked themselves why God had allowed them to be so harshly punished. Their answer was that it was because of their unfaithfulness. Their response: they would no longer allow themselves to be influenced by other cultures and their gods. Men who had married foreign women must divorce them. Strict adherence to the laws of God was to be assured by an extensive set of commandments that covered every aspect of life. Further, contact with Gentiles, or non-Jews, was to be kept at a minimum. Thus, Pharisaic Judaism was born.

Yet they soon found that it is difficult or perhaps impossible to keep isolated from the inroads of other cultures. The new threat was that of the Greeks, or Hellenes, coming into their territory by the military inroads of Alexander the Great. He had inherited the Greek city-states, which his father had conquered. He himself loved Hellenic civilization. Even today we too are often amazed at what these Greeks accomplished: in architecture, in literature and the theater, and especially in philosophy. Socrates, Plato, and Aristotle are still admired and are read today.

Alexander quickly proved himself to be a great general when he invaded and easily defeated the long-standing enemies of the Greeks, the Persians. From there he conquered much of the Middle East, including Israel.

Alexander, as enamored as he was by Greek culture, intentionally left numerous cites around his empire as centers from which that culture could spread. They were all named, understandably, Alexandria. Upon his death his empire was divided up, with the family of the Seleucids receiving the share that included Israel. Its later ruler was Antioch Epiphanes, called the Enlighted One.

The American Jesus?

He decided to spread Hellenism, Greek culture, as a gift throughout his kingdom, and to enforce it on all who would resist it. This included the Jews, who had recently decided to resist all foreign influences. He ordered all Jewish priests to sacrifice to pagan gods. One of these priests killed the messenger of the king, and the War of the Maccabees was on.

One can only admire the faith and the grit of this small Jewish nation that held off the might of the powerful kingdom for about one hundred years, fiercely resisting Hellenic culture with its pagan aspects. Eventually, the Jews even recaptured Jerusalem.

Yet success can produce division, and it did so here. Various factions arose, each vying for control. One of these groups decided to call in Rome for help. And where Rome comes in, Rome does not leave! Palestine became part of the ever-growing Roman Empire, which by the addition of that land now controlled much of the Mediterranean, which they referred to as *mare nostrum*, or "Our Lake." They had already made Greece a part of their empire, and Greek thinking had its influence among the conquerors as well as the conquered.

By the time of Jesus, Palestine was a cultural hodgepodge. Jews tried to maintain their identity while being ruled by Rome, in a world largely influenced by Greek thinking.

Jesus himself seems to have remained faithful to the Mosaic Law, but insisted on applying it to the inner person, decrying those who were only interested in cleaning the outer rim of the cup while the inside remained filthy. He also broke through the isolated approach of the Pharisees, often dealing with Gentiles and welcoming sinners.

For his troubles, Jesus was crucified by the combined forces of the two most powerful cultures of his world: Roman and Jewish.

The biblical history is filled with cultural conflicts. So is the entire history of the church. As we shall see in further chapters, the early church was forced to deal with its surrounding culture, and so have Christians throughout history. Yet we now return to modern America to take a look at some of the cultural challenges the church faces today.

Introduction
CHRISTIANS IN AMERICA

Every Christian lives in some culture. And every culture necessarily has some virtues to it, or it could not flourish. The question for Christians at any time is what aspects of their milieu are compatible with Christian faith and morality.

What then are the major aspects of our American culture, and to what extent do they enhance Christian living or make it more difficult?

A Question of Basics

For any worthwhile examination of whether the American culture (or any culture, for that matter) is compatible with Christian life and teachings, it seems necessary to ask two questions: First, what are the irreducible basics of Christianity? And second, what are the basic beliefs and life patterns of that society?

Grace

It is not at all far-fetched to believe that the concept of the grace of God is central to the Scriptures and especially to the New Testament. The Greek term for grace is *charis*, is evidently derived from *chairo*, "to look favorably upon" or "to take delight in." The concept in the New Testament is that God looks favorably on us, even when that favor is undeserved. It is an undeserved gift, an unearned blessing. It bestows on one what he or she has not deserved.

> Amazing grace, how sweet the sound,
> that saved a wretch like me.[4]

The concept of undeserved grace is also found throughout the Old Testament.

The prophets continually scold the Hebrew people, who, although called and blessed by God without their merit, still remained stiff-necked and rebellious.

---
4. John Newton, "Amazing Grace" (1772).

The American Jesus?

In the exodus, God takes them out of slavery, although they had done nothing to deserve it. Even the Ten Commandments assume his previous activities. These laws are premised in the first word, which reminds them that he had already freed them from slavery, and so in response they must be obedient.

When the Israelites became unfaithful and corrupt, the prophets continually harped on their sins, but in most cases they insisted that after well-deserved punishment, God would rescue a remnant. Hosea proclaims that God will take back his people, just as the prophet himself takes back his unfaithful wife.

Those returning from exile saw that return as a gift from God, which placed upon them the responsibility of obedience.

Throughout the Psalms there is the recurring theme of trust in God's gracious forgiveness from sin and help in times of trouble.

But it is in the New Testament that grace clearly becomes central. *Charis* in one form or another is used over 150 times, usually expressing the theme of God's favor.

Luke tells us that Mary "found favor" with God. The child Jesus "found favor" with God and man.

Jesus himself stresses the gracious nature of the Heavenly Father, who forgives the sinner. Jesus dines with the Pharisee and the publican and welcomes home the prodigal.

The prologue to John connects grace with Jesus Christ himself. He is "full of grace and truth" (John 1:14). "From his fullness we have received grace upon grace" (1:16) And, "The law came through Moses, but grace and truth through Jesus Christ" (1:17).

Yet by far the most excited proclaimer of the grace of God coming in Jesus was Paul. Time and time again he expresses joy in his discovery of the grace of God in Jesus Christ, or better, that this grace had discovered him: "By grace you have been saved through faith. And this is not your own doing. It is a gift of God" (Eph 2:8).

But Paul did not come to this realization easily. He tells us he was "a Pharisee of the Pharisees," evidently trusting in his own righteousness according to the law, which he evidently kept scrupulously. He was first an opponent of the new faith, joining in the killing of Steven. Yet it was on a journey to persecute Christians

Introduction

that he experienced the presence of Christ, and was converted to the new faith, for which he became one of its greatest advocates, traveling extensively to proclaim it.

Every writing of Paul rings with his joy in this faith, trusting in the favor of God, and not in his own piety. Nowhere is this clearer than in his Letter to the Romans, a kind of summary of his message. It is in the third chapter of this book that he sums up his message.

Paul, ever the Pharisee, feels it necessary to ask what advantage there is in being a Jew. "Much!," he insists, because the Jew is entrusted with God's word. But all, Jew and Gentile, are both under the power of sin.

What the law does is expose our sin and make us accountable. It does not justify us before God (make us just in his eyes). Rather, it shows us that we are not made acceptable by the law, only held accountable by it.

How then can any of us be justified? "We are now justified by his grace as a gift, through the redemption that is in Christ Jesus ..." (Rom 3:24). God's righteousness is shown in that he makes us righteous! This is made possible by faith, not by the law; faith in God's graciousness, not in ourselves.

For Paul, the great example of this in the Hebrew Scriptures is not Moses, the lawgiver, but Abraham, the man of faith: "Abraham believed God, and it was reckoned to him as righteousness" (Rom 4:1–15). It is not by works that we are accepted by God as righteous, but by faith, or as we saw earlier, belief or trust.

This dynamic view of our relation to God totally reverses much of our usual understanding of religion. It is trusting in God, not in our own virtue or accomplishments.

Paul's radical understanding of faith had enormous cultural consequences. As a Jew who now saw his Judaism in a new light, he went from synagogue to synagogue proclaiming Christ. Sometimes he was accepted, sometimes not. Occasionally Gentiles were interested. But it was in Antioch of Pisidia that an immense change came (Acts 13). Being rejected by the Jews there, he proclaimed that he would now turn to the Gentiles. Now one of the most

The American Jesus?

dedicated and energetic of early Christians would devote himself to proclaiming the Good News to non-Jews.

Paul's hope that it is God's grace and not the law that will open the door for non-Jews to enter the faith, with the accompanying difficult questions about how their cultural beliefs and practices will, or will not, facilitate their new faith. This problem is still with us.

American Basics

If God's grace is an irreducible aspect of Christianity, a sine qua non of the faith, what are the basics of the American way of life, its own sine qua non, that without which it would not be what it is? I will explore five characteristics of the American faith, the American belief system, and seek to relate or contrast them to God's grace, if and when it is possible.

The first thing that comes to mind about America is what has been our innate *optimism*. We are the "can do!" people. This can account for much of our success in the political realm as well as in the sciences and engineering. If there is a problem, it is there to be solved.

This often includes an optimism about ourselves, our basic goodness, and the goodness of our goals. The question that necessarily arises is to what extent this is compatible with the biblical and traditional Christian teachings about grace.

Nowhere is this issue more obvious than in the preaching of Joel Osteen. He is at this time among the most influential of American TV preachers. His books are best-sellers. Immense crowds come to hear him in person. Clearly, his message resonates with something in the American psyche.[5]

To his credit, he proclaims God's love for us all. He also insists on the need for personal integrity, honesty, selflessness, and sharing with others—something not always observable in many modern clerics.

---

5. E.g., Osteen, *Your Best Life Now.*

Introduction

Yet the heart of his message and the greater part of his appeal is his positive thinking. In this he stands in the tradition of Norman Vincent Peale and Robert Schuller. He offers a salutary antidote to guilt-ridden lives and philosophical cynicism. It is precisely here that he is most in keeping with American optimism, but he may be proclaiming a cultural belief while at the same time denying what is central to the New Testament and the great thrust of Christian tradition: sin and the need for grace.

To begin, it seems apparent that Osteen's faith is that God wants for you exactly what you already want for yourself. God wants the best for you. He wants to make life easier for you, and to give you an advantage. He wants to give you the desires of your heart. He wants you to be complete and content: a good marriage, happiness, and abundance.

Our response to this, he says, is faith. This means seeing yourself on a new level. It means believing that your business will take off, that you will prosper financially. Setting your mind on higher things is seeing yourself as stronger, healthier, and victorious. It involves believing that you will get that promotion. It believes that you can get that house that you seemingly cannot afford, just as the Osteens obtained the huge stadium in which they now worship. So then pray! Have faith that God will get you customers.

It appears that there is little or none of the offense of Christianity left here. While God affirms our personal values, it is hard to find anywhere that he confronts them or holds them in question.

While Osteen insists that our success in life is ultimately by God's grace, he also says that if you do your part, God will do his part. If you keep the right (i.e., positive) attitude, he will repay you double for your trouble. Behind this is the belief in the innate goodness of us all.

It is no accident that Osteen seldom mentions sin. This may have a positive side, since for so many preachers sin is whether you smoke, drink, or swear. He knows his Bible well enough to say that sin is "missing the mark." But Osteen's heart is surely elsewhere. A positive attitude toward ourselves, our goals, and God's approval of us is his dearest belief. While God forgives us, it is more often for mistakes we make, with little awareness that there a deep spiritual disease in the human heart—except, perhaps, for negative thinking, which may be for Osteen something close to the ultimate sin.

It is also telling that he very seldom mentions Jesus. We can well understand why this is so. It is not surprising. Why would we need Jesus? We certainly do not need the Jesus of Luther, who stands between us and the Father's wrath, nor the Jesus of Augustine, who brings healing to our deep disorientation.

The cross is simply not mentioned. In the more than three hundred pages of *Your Best Life Now*, there is only one reference to Jesus giving his life. And this is in another context.

It is clear that Osteen's message is both appropriate and appealing to a culture that wants to think positively, and strongly resents any hint that we who are part of it may ourselves be infected with hopes and desires that can warp and distort our very beings and our relationships with other persons and cultures. What we have here is clearly a matter of American positive thinking: a la Peale, Schuller, and, of course, Osteen himself. Russell Moore is certainly right when he suggests that these thinkers "are more akin to a Canaanite fertility religion than to the gospel of Jesus Christ."[6] That is, our relationship to God is one where we attempt to gain the most we can from him.

One serious problem that arises when the Christian faith is reduced to positive thinking is the problem of evil. We refer here not to the evils that beset us all simply due to the fact that we are human and mortal. The problem for Christians is that we are called to suffer because we are Christians, and we are sometimes called to take stands and act in ways that are counter to our culture. Old Testament prophets were often rejected. Jeremiah was called "the weeping prophet." Jesus himself was crucified by the powers that ruled. He admonished his followers to take up their cross, and told them that he would bring not peace, but a sword. Paul, a persecutor himself, was then himself persecuted. Many early believers felt the wrath of Rome. In our own day, believers who feel that their faith puts them in opposition to their cultural zeitgeist of the

---

6. Moore, *Onward*, 64.

Introduction

day have found suffering in their paths: witness Christians under Stalin and Hitler, as well as Americans who have fought for equal rights, and on and on.

It is wonderful when believers can live out their lives honestly in their culture, but all too often belief brings antagonism with society, and the accompanying suffering that attends it. On the other hand, many of us may avoid suffering for our faith by being all too willing to turn our eyes away from the false gods and the injustices around us.

A second aspect of American thinking that is observed by almost all is *pragmatism*, a philosophy that is uninterested in theoretical musings, but only concerned with what works. We are a practical people! In fact, we totally reject as impractical any abstractions that offer no worthwhile results.

It is interesting that America has until recently never adopted the many philosophies emanating from Europe. And the only philosophy that we have ever developed on our own is pragmatism. Probably its most important advocate has been John Dewey. He actually preferred to have his views labeled as "instrumentalism." Here, the mind is seen as an instrument that makes it possible for us to survive in the best possible way. He explains that the only relevant question to ask is what real effects will result from an action or belief. In one of his writings he offers this analogy: Imagine that you are going somewhere, but on your walk you find that the way is blocked by a huge gulf in the road. What do you do? You may think about jumping across, going around, placing a board over the gulf. Which is the correct answer? The one that works!

This philosophy has been a hugely successful way of thinking for Americans. It is largely responsible for the almost unbelievable progress we have made in science, technology, and economics.

But many thinkers, Christian and otherwise, have found it lacking in some important ways. For one thing, while it can get you "there," it does little or nothing to guide you in what "there" is. Unless I know where I am going, how will I know what is really getting me there? Most of us have some idea, perhaps unexamined, of

The American Jesus?

where we want to go: to be president, discover the cure for cancer, get rich, or something else. Pragmatism gives us no guidance here.

Another problem that I encounter as a human being, where pragmatism might disappoint me, is that I must face the fact it is not only my surroundings, but also my own inner orientation, that keeps me from doing what is best practically. However noble my goals may be, my inner fears and disorientation may keep me from realizing them. Or they may actually twist me into seeking goods that are harmful.

In these regards, American pragmatism may see Christianity simply as a tool to achieve success, no matter how that success is defined or understood.

Another aspect of the American experience is *pluralism*. Historically, we have attracted a menagerie of peoples from elsewhere, as few nations on Earth have done. We have welcomed, or at least tolerated, nationalities and religions from everywhere. "Give me your tired and your poor, your huddled masses yearning to breathe free." We have made a home for persecuted cultures and religions, and for the most part have been able to integrate them, and "Americanize" them into our society. This stands at the core of our national greatness.

But this laudable success has come at a price. So many peoples living and working peacefully together has meant that certain values must be adjusted, or even abandoned, to keep peace.

We can now look at two additional views of our national life that help us to survive at an optimum level: *relativism* and *secularism*. To what extent these are compatible with any kind of Christianity is questionable.

Relativism: In order to "get along" in a society that welcomes and contains so many different lifestyles and religions, Christian and other, it seems appropriate to adopt a kind of relativism. This approach maintains that no truth is absolute. All can claim only relative truth. It is also consistent with the basic American democratic creed that each person has the right to make up his or her own mind on important issues.

Introduction

This way of dealing with our multi-everything nation has a generous and salutary humility to it. Yet it also contains its own absolutism: anyone who questions the belief that all truths are relative must be rejected as questioning the absolute truth of relativism. Christians often face just this accusation, because there are some things we hold as true, simply true.

Although most Americans seem content to rest secure in just such a position, it is hard to see how, rather than uniting us, it may just as well lead to intellectual chaos, where "ignorant armies clash by night," and there are no common beliefs that can bring us together. The case can be made that it is just such kinds of beliefs that were helpless in the face of demonic tyrannies in the form of Hitler's Nazism and Stalin's communism.

This leads to another set of beliefs that are common in America, and throughout much of the Western, formerly Christian, world: *secularism*. The modern history of the Western world is fraught with horrible examples of religious persecutions and religious wars, many of them in the name of the Prince of Peace. It is enough to drive any decent person away from all religious belief, and to place one's hope and faith in what the world and society have to offer.

"Secular" is from the Latin *saeculum*, which refers to the present age, usually to the exclusion of any religious beliefs and practices. Faith in science, social progress, and the innate goodness of the human race are the usual substitutes. In Europe, the grandest cathedrals, from another age, stand empty, while attempts at progress in other areas of life go on apace.

In the United States the First Amendment to the Constitution states that congress shall pass no law establishing any religion. Although the term "separation of church and state" is not in the Constitution, it has become the basic understanding of that amendment.

The idea that government has no business meddling in religious matters has allowed religions of all sorts to flourish here. It is one of the pillars of our democratic society.

In his book *The Secular City*, Harvey Cox rejoices that we are now free from religious dogmas being injected into the body

The American Jesus?

politic. We can now "get the ghost out of the machine," taking the world on its own terms, unconcerned with placating the gods and spirits thought to be in it.

Cox sees his position as thoroughly in keeping with the Old Testament prophets, who were continually opposing the religions of their day, and mocking the various gods who dominated people's lives, while these deities were really mere nothings. Thus, they freed the people from the fears and burdens that these gods brought.[7]

American secularism has been a truly positive aspect of our society and our lives, and especially in its ability to allow religions of all sorts to prosper.

But on the other side of the coin, there is the question of whether secularism itself has not become its own religion, its own ultimate, which can be as demanding and oppressive as any other religion. Christian beliefs and practices are more and more excluded from the public square at the same time that governments—national, state, and local—are dominating a greater and greater share of our lives. It remains to be seen what effects for good or evil this will have on both church and state.

LOOKING FORWARD

The American experiment in social life, politics, and religion has been an undeniable success in many regards. It has allowed individuals to practice, or to ignore, whatever faith they desire. It has engendered a huge and confusing variety of religious life and thought. Freedom from politicians and priests has produced one of the most productive and exciting panoramas anywhere or at any other time.

On my shelf is a book titled *Americanism: The Fourth Great Western Religion*, by David Gelernter.[8] It puts forth the idea that Judaism was true in its way but was surpassed by Catholicism. In turn, Catholicism was surpassed by Protestantism. Finally, Americanism comes, which surpasses them all. It is truly *the* great religion.

---

7. Cox, *Secular City*.
8. Gelernter, *Americanism*.

Introduction

The question, of course, is not whether American beliefs and practices surpass previous incarnations of Christianity, but how the two are related. This brings us back to our original question of whether Christianity is the same thing as Americanism, or whether they are incompatible, or perhaps overlap in some ways.

In order to deal with this issue, we must look at various expressions of the faith, as seen, of course, in the Bible. But it is also important to look at some of the most seminal theologies throughout time and place, and relate them to Paul's "faith, hope, and love."

Faith is basic to all believers. Certainly, one of the great advocates of this is Martin Luther. It will be necessary to examine his experience of this faith.

Christians have always clung to some manner of hope in the face of doubt and despair. Irenaeus of Lyon, from the second century, will be our guide here.

Perhaps the greatest articulation of divine and human love in the history of the church is from Augustine of Hippo. We will look at his beliefs.

In looking at them we can unfold for ourselves some of the depths and riches of the Christian faith and examine ourselves and our culture in that light.

1

Faith (1)

Abraham believed God, and it was reckoned to him as righteousness.

—GEN 15:6; ROM 4:3

Trust in the Lord with all your heart.

—PROV 3:5

THE BIBLICAL BACKGROUND AND CHRISTIANITY

ANY ATTEMPT TO UNDERSTAND what Christianity is all about must clearly begin with a look at what faith means in the Scriptures. After all, Christianity is often rightly referred to as the Christian *faith*. We will also follow some of the historical twists and turns of Christian history and notice how that faith and various cultures sometimes collide.

It is clear that the Old Testament prophets were continually calling on the leaders and people to trust in the Lord, rather than in their own powers and cleverness, or in kings. In the New Testament, faith clearly takes central place. The Greek term *pistis*, or "faith," is used over 270 times. *Pisteuo*, or "to be persuaded," occurs

Faith (1)

at least 220 times. Sometimes the term simply refers to belief that something is true. But far more often it is a conviction or trust by which a person is impelled to action by an inner principle. It is used especially of a faith by which a person trusts Jesus, i.e., a confidence in him combined with obedience to him and/or faith in the Father; the giving up of oneself to him.

This latter usage is basic to the New Testament and is found virtually everywhere. The centurion is told to go. His servant was healed according to the centurion's faith (Matt 8:13).

Jesus said the people did not believe in him because they did not believe in the one who sent him (John 5:38). Of course, we cannot omit the famous faith passage in the eleventh chapter of Hebrews. "By faith our ancestors received approval . . . By faith Abel offered a more acceptable sacrifice . . . By faith Enoch was taken so he did not see death," and the author goes on through the whole Old testament, leading up to Jesus (Hebrews 11).

But as we have seen, it is Paul who was the great champion of faith in the New Testament. It was faith, not human effort, that was central to our relation to God: "salvation through faith in Jesus Christ" (2 Tim 3:13); "yet we know that a person is justified not by works of the law but through faith in Jesus Christ" (Gal 2:16). And again, "for Christ is the end of the law so that there may be righteousness for everyone who believes" (Rom 10:4).

It is important to notice at this point that Paul never proclaims that no law is to be observed by the believer. For him it is not a matter of either trust or obedience to the law. Rather, it is a matter of both/and. Trust is the basis of obedience, not a substitute for it.

THE EARLY CHURCH

As we have seen, Paul's insistence that God's grace is given through faith allowed him to break free of his Jewish cocoon and present a message that transcended a narrow Jewish worldview. As a result of his work and that of others, the early church was able to make its breakout into the wider, Greco-Roman world, offering God's grace

The American Jesus?

to all who believed, Gentiles as well as pious Jews. Yet this also brought with it, not only new opportunities, but also new threats. [1]

At this time, the early church was being subjected to attack from both Roman political opposition and Greek intellectual criticism, even ridicule. First, the political opposition: That Rome was open to new religious ideas and sects is obvious if one only looks at the Pantheon, where gods from all over the empire were represented. But these same Romans were also particularly afraid of new religions, which could serve as masks for subversive groups. Christianity was new! How could Christians defend themselves? They could attempt to say that they were authentic Judaism, but during this period these very Jews were in rebellion against Rome.

But the issue was even deeper than fear of subversion. Rome could keep order by allowing all of these religions to exist together at the same time. So, there was relativism there for the sake of political order. But this was really a kind of absolutized relativism. If any group, such as the Christians, insisted that their beliefs were true, and simply that, then Roman "tolerance" would come down upon them in the name of tolerance, a reaction not entirely unknown in our own culture.

In the face of persecution, the Christians might simply insist that they were good Romans, never wanting to rebel against the powers that be. A host of Christian thinkers, known as the apologists, tried to defend their new faith in just such a way against Roman traditionalism. Christians were accused of being unpatriotic. The response: we are good citizens, but we do have a higher loyalty, to God. Another accusation: they were immoral; since non-believers were not allowed to be present at their Eucharist, something untoward must be going on. They answered that they were the most moral of Romans, since they knew that the eye of God was upon them.

One of the main accusations against them was that they were stupid! After all, Rome had inherited the great thoughts and thinkers of the Greeks. Christians had no such background

---

1. The general history of early Christianity can be found in a number of church histories, such as Walker, *History of the Christian Church*.

Faith (1)

about which they could boast. Of course, the stupidity charge is an accusation that has been brought against believers for centuries, including today. How could they respond? One defender, Justin, writing in the middle of the second century, attempted to mount just such a defense.

Justin did not ridicule Greek thinking. Far from it! In fact, he insisted that one of the schools of philosophy of the day was true. This was Stoicism, one of the schools that the Romans had taken over from the Greeks.

The Stoics believed in a god. Not the god who created the world, but the god who *was* the world! For them, god is what is! Stoicism had some popularity in the empire at that time and was even espoused by some emperors. Stoics not only believed that god is the same as the universe, but that he is rational, so the universe is rational. Their term for this rational organization of the world, the mind of god, was *Logos*, or "Word." Our words are the expression of our inner logic; so also, the rational organization of the universe is god's word.

All great thinkers, such as Socrates, the Stoics said, have had some of this word within them. But the Word in its fullness has only come, said Justin, in Jesus, whom the Gospel of John tells us was "the Word made flesh dwelling among us, full of grace and truth." Thus, Justin tried to unite the message of Christianity with some of the best of classical thinking. His ideas were not accepted by that same classical world. In fact, he was executed for his faith. His full title is Justin Martyr. The culture of his day was not ready to hear his message.

In fact, for the first two centuries, Christians were often martyred for their faith. Sometimes persecutions were general, throughout the empire, instigated by one emperor or another. But sometimes they were simply the result of mob violence. Yet Christians never had secure footing in their new cultural world.

While the earliest Christians found themselves at odds with their own culture, the Jewish, now they were also rejected and persecuted by their new broader culture, the Greco-Roman.

The American Jesus?

Yet during the same period the empire itself was also suffering hard times. There was little if any stability at the top. One emperor after another arose from the military ranks and was quickly overthrown by another. In one sixty-nine-year period, from AD 235 to 284, there were twenty-six emperors, the so-called barracks emperors. Something had to be done! Diocletian, the last of them, decided to reorganize the empire and give it stability. He appointed three other emperors: two would be for the east and two for the west. In each part, one would be the emperor and the other would be his second, ready to take over if the leader was gone, thus ensuring stability. As part of his revitalization plan, he also persecuted Christians.

It seemed to be a good plan, but it did not work. Very soon many were fighting each other for the purple, and still others joined in. By the year 325 four generals were fighting: two in the west and two in the east. The western combatants were Maxentius at Rome, a persecutor, and Constantine, who did not persecute Christians, and was to some extent favorably disposed to the faith.

As Constantine related it, on the eve of the battle between their two forces, he saw in the sky the Greek letters *chi* and *rho*, the first two letters of "Christ." Around them were the words "in this sign conquer." He had his soldiers put these letters on their shields. In the ensuing battle Constantine won! Understandably, he attributed his victory to the Christian God.

Thus came about a major shift in the relations of church and state, faith and culture. It was a shift that was to affect Christian life and its relation to its surrounding culture for centuries, with some echoes of it present even today.

Constantine now favored the church in various ways. He met with Licinius, the victor in the east, and together they issued the Edict of Milan, which decreed religious liberty for all, but particularly singled out Christians for protection. Constantine eventually defeated Licinius and became the sole emperor of the empire: its first Christian emperor.

Faith (1)

Christians were now in a new world, where they were favored rather than abused. It is understandable that many Christians, escaping persecution, were overjoyed at this new situation. Some even likened Constantine to a kind of second, political Christ.

But this new situation was a two-edged sword. The same emperor who saved you can also control you. While Constantine favored some, he also persecuted others. While most Christians were delighted with this new situation, others were not so sure, wondering whether Christ had been sold out to Caesar.

THE ARIAN CONTROVERSY

The new situation also led to other issues, including even how one should think about Jesus Christ himself. The Arian controversy was a prime example of this. It divided the entire empire, with one group believing that Christ was truly divine, and should be worshipped as such, while the other held that the Word in Christ may well be the highest of creatures, but only a creature nonetheless. Arius could not believe that Jesus was truly divine. It seems that he clothed his theology in the philosophy of Aristotle. Aristotle had believed in a god, but a god that was so perfect that he could not be affected by the changes going on in the world. God was the "self-thinking thought," blissfully unaware of whatever was beneath him. It was somewhat like a beautiful woman attracting all men to herself, but unaware of any of them and not subject to change by them. Since Jesus was involved in the world of change, the Word in Jesus must change, and so cannot be divine. So said Arius.

Arius was opposed by others, such as Athanasius, the archbishop of Alexandria, whose concern was not so much philosophical, but theological. His position was that we desperately need salvation. Only God can save. So, if Christ is to save us, he must be God.[2]

Although it might be hard for us today to understand the depth of feeling engendered by this issue, the Roman world was

---

2. See Athanasius, *Against Heresies*.

The American Jesus?

rent apart over it, and Constantine saw that the spiritual glue of his empire was coming apart. Nothing seemed to heal the schism. So the emperor, not yet even baptized, called a council of bishops at Nicea in 325 to resolve the issue. He himself attended. The council decided for the full divinity of Christ, as expressed in its creed, the Nicene, still used by liturgical churches today.

Constantine took the novel step of exiling those who refused to comply. This is the first example of a Christian emperor punishing Christians for wrong beliefs. Later, he came under the influence of an Arian bishop, and exiled some Nicenes! The handwriting was on the wall for the future. Now the very things we believe about Jesus will be entangled with questions of faith and culture, church and state.

This debate clearly illustrates how entangled all of these elements can get, church and state, philosophy and theology, the great thoughts of a culture and questions of salvation.

It seems that whenever Christians are in a privileged position, they start fighting over practices and are also often confronted with cultural and philosophical issues as well. The decrees resulting from some of these controversies, as in Nicea, actually split the church with schisms, some of which have lasted until today.

Observation: Battles over theology, entangled with political issues, have raged for centuries. Sometimes popes and bishops will get the upper hand. At other times it will be nobles or kings. Eventually, the Americans separated the two in the great American experiment, which attempts to keep church and state separate.

But now new issues have arisen, which we have not necessarily worked out well, since the problem is often deeper than simply church and state. It is a matter of faith and culture. Can any culture survive with no spiritual glue to hold it together? Or, conversely, do we now really have a state religion, or highest spiritual value, called relativism or secularism, where all faiths are considered to be equal before the law, and are perhaps also believed to be equal before God himself?

Faith (1)

AUGUSTINE AND THE PELAGIAN CONTROVERSY

At its heart, one way or another, the basic question has always concerned one's faith in Jesus Christ. Never was this clearer than in the debate between Augustine and Pelagius. It is at heart a serious debate about human nature. Are we called by God to make use of our own God-given moral abilities to seek the perfection that is our due? Or are we called, rather, to recognize our spiritual and moral weakness, and place our faith, not in our own virtues, but in God's totally undeserved grace?

The Eastern Church has produced many notable "fathers." But in the Western, Latin-speaking church one thinker stands out above the others: Augustine of Hippo (d. AD 430). Happily, he tells us about his own early spiritual development, his journal to faith, in his autobiographical *Confessions*.[3]

He was born in North Africa, then still a part of the Roman Empire. From early on, he was seen as being particularly bright. He was sent to Carthage to study rhetoric, at that time one of the ways to the top in the empire. He excelled in his studies. Meanwhile he was sexually active. He tells us that this prayer at that time was, "Lord, make me chaste, but not yet!" Intellectually, he was attracted to the Manicheans, a very dualistic sect. He eventually lost faith in their teachings but remained a member for years.

Meanwhile, he was more and more successful in his career, gaining a position as professor of rhetoric at Milan, at times the functional capital of the Western empire. Yet, despite all this, he was unhappy. He could not find the truths he sought to satisfy his soul. But one day, he tells us, someone placed in his hands some "books of the Platonists," perhaps the works of Plotinus, a leading Neoplatonic philosopher of the day. He found in them the truths he sought and remained a Platonist throughout his life. Yet the influence of his mother, a devout Christian, was still with him. He said that in those books there was one thing lacking. There was no mention of "the Word made flesh." He still had some searching to do. In fact, spiritually, he was miserable.

---

3 See Brown, *Augustine*.

The American Jesus?

He gradually moved closer and closer to the Christian faith, often under the influence of Ambrose, bishop of Milan. But it was during a visit from a friend that he came to see his need to make the necessary decision for Christ. He tells us that in the garden of Milan he read the scripture, "Put on the Lord Jesus Christ, and make no provision for the flesh." He said he read no further, nor needed to. He was converted.

Augustine resigned his position, which had demanded that he teach his students how to lie, a technique often practiced up until today. With some friends, he began to live a kind of monastic/philosophical life.

But this was interrupted when, on a trip to Hippo Regius in North Africa, during a worship service, the congregation recognized this famous person in their midst. They forcibly pushed him forward to be their new priest. Later he became their bishop, and from this city he held conferences, preached and wrote, dominating much of Western thinking.

Later, as he looked over what had happened to him, he could not help but see that he had resisted God all along, but that God had continually arranged things so that he, Augustine, could never be happy until he turned to God. That is to say, his conversion was not his doing. In fact, it was against his will, until God finally triumphed. It was all grace! From now on, all of his teaching and writing would be based on this premise. Much later, the Middle Ages gave him the title "Doctor of Grace."

For Augustine, in our natural state we are really not free, but bound. Our wills are turned in on ourselves. Only the grace of God can free us from this native selfishness.[4]

Not everyone agreed with his strong emphasis on a faith that trusted in God, and in God alone, for our salvation. There were other influences and other teachers in the Christian world at the time. One of these teachers was Pelagius, a devout monk from Ireland who had moved to Rome, where he taught and encouraged others to take on the holy life. While Augustine was preaching and writing about the primacy of God's grace in the Christian life,

---

4. See Augustine, *To Simplician* 1.2.2; and *On the Spirit and the Letter* 5.

Faith (1)

Pelagius' whole message stressed human responsibility and human initiative in our relation to God.

Pelagius insisted that we are completely capable of making this choice. Any thought that we cannot do it was simply an excuse. He was always ready with the encouraging word, "Yes you can!"

In a letter to young woman, Demetrias,[5] Pelagius explains that we are like a coin that has the image of the king on it. It can be grimed over, so the image is not seen. But with a little polish, that image will shine through. We all have the image of God in us, he says, but it has become dirtied by sin. Yet, with the polish of the law, it will again shine through.

God made us good, he said, and it is even possible to achieve moral perfection, as some biblical saints had clearly done. Adam sinned, not by giving us some inborn corruption, but only as a bad example for us to imitate. On the other hand, we also have the examples of many saints, and especially of Jesus himself. He is the king of law, incarnate.

Pelagius does believe in grace, but for him it is simply the gift of our natural goodness, the law, the examples of the saints, and especially of Jesus himself. Nowhere in Pelagius do we find the desperate moral and spiritual struggle that Augustine had endured.

Pelagius had read in Augustine's *Confessions* the prayer, "Give what you demand, and demand what you will!" He believed that Augustine meant that we can only do what God demands if God gives us the gift of his power to do it. This ran counter to everything Pelagius believed about our own freedom and responsibility. Of course, Pelagius was right in reading it that way.

Meanwhile, the barbarian Visigoths were threatening Italy, and many citizens fled south to Africa. So did Pelagius and his friend Coelestius. They even passed through Hippo, but when Coelestius applied for ordination, he was denied. The African Christians charged him with believing, among other things, that babies are born sinless, in Adam's original state, and that the law

---

5. Pelagius, *Letter to Demetrias*, in Pelagius, *Letters*. This letter was often mistakenly thought to be from the pen of St. Jerome.

The American Jesus?

is as good as the Gospel for salvation. He refused to respond. The two men headed east, Pelagius to Palestine.

A trial was held concerning Pelagius in Jerusalem. He was charged with teaching that a person can live without sin, easily. He responded that one needs grace. Of course, for him, grace merely meant free will, the law, and good examples. At another trial, in Diospolis, he himself condemned the charges made against him and was acquitted. Augustine said that by acquitting the man they really condemned the doctrines.

Several trials were held that also condemned him, and even the pope, who had originally approved of Pelagius, eventually agreed.

In the debates it became clear what the basic issues were. For Pelagius and his followers, the major issue was that moral endeavor was essential. If we are truly infected with sin, as Augustine taught, this endeavor would be impossible, and it also would cut the cord of all moral striving. For Augustine, the matter was to admit the sorry state of humanity, inherited from Adam, which could only be remedied by grace. Pelagius placed too much faith in himself, Augustine said, and not in God. To deny the illness is to deny the divine remedy. Grace is not nature but is given to a corrupted nature through Jesus Christ. That is where faith in Christ is necessary.[6]

Others who were not Pelagians were troubled by Augustine's emphasis on grace. Some monks, who believed it was helpful to correct one another for their salvation, complained that Augustine's views about grace made us totally passive. If he is correct, why admonish one another? In fact, why do anything at all? Augustine responded that grace is not given in response to our choices, but our good choices themselves are the result of the free gift of grace.

For Augustine, it is the unearned grace of Christ that is our hope, not our own goodness or efforts.

---

6. See Augustine, *On Nature and Grace* 3.

Faith (1)

INTERIM

Officially, Augustine won the battle over grace. His views were affirmed by a number of councils. But in fact Pelagianism was still there. Even those who considered themselves to be true Augustinians often held a mixture of Pelagius' ideas. This would persist as the generations rolled on. We might even suggest that this Pelagianism is present in the American "can do" spirit as applied to religious matters.

Politically and socially, the situation would soon change drastically. The invading Visigoths were followed by other marauding tribes: the Ostrogoths, Vandals, Burgundians, Sueves, and more. Every part of the empire was affected. The last Roman emperor in the West, Romulus, was deposed in 475, just thirty years after the bishop of Hippo's death, and Romulus was not replaced.

The classical civilization of Greece and Rome was at an end in the West. The Middle Ages, the age of faith and of chaos, had begun. Western Christianity, which had tied its fate to that civilization, fell on hard times. Often the only force capable of offering any order to life was the church, perhaps the local bishop and the monks. The pope at Rome became one of the few forces to which one could look for order. Thus, in the midst of chaos, the church, in a strange way, began to take center stage in the West.

In this difficult atmosphere there were occasional attempts at learning and scholarship, as in the Carolingian Renaissance of the early ninth century. But this fell apart in light of the Viking invasions.

Yet there was another political and social rebirth in the thirteenth century. It produced one of the great minds in the Western church, Thomas Aquinas. He was able to set out a consistent view of the faith. During his time, the West was relearning about the views of Aristotle. Augustine had couched his Christian teachings in the best philosophy of his day, that of Plato. Thomas did it with Aristotle, showing us that it is possible to understand our faith in differing intellectual ways, without, perhaps, sacrificing its inner core.

The American Jesus?

Thomas was a faithful Augustinian but expressed that faith in Aristotelian terms. He was also able to apply these teachings to the culture of that day.

His way of uniting his faith to the new cultural/intellectual situation was to accept the four classical Greek virtues of wisdom, justice, courage, and temperance. But on top of these he placed the specific Christian virtue of faith. Christian faith permeates the four and gives them a newer and higher meaning. As we shall see, for Thomas, even faith was itself permeated by the even higher, God-given virtues of hope and love.[7]

Thomas was one of the great influences of the time, but his influence tended to wane, particularly, under the influence of important cultural changes. The Middle Ages were dying, and the Renaissance had begun, with new thoughts, a kind of fresh air, which challenged not only some important church teachings, but even the structures of society itself.

MARTIN LUTHER AND THE PROTESTANT REFORMATION

I have swept away your transgressions like a cloud,
And your sins like mist;
Return to me, for I have redeemed you.

—Isa 44:22

Martin Luther was born in Germany in 1483.[8] It was a time when medieval institutions were still strong, but new ideas were already floating in the air. He had originally intended to study for the law, but experienced an abrupt change for his own life, which also would have a profound effect on the whole of Western culture.

---

7. Thomas, *Summa Theologica*, q. 112, art. 1, 2 and q. 113, 1, 2, *et passim*. Found in Thomas, *Basic Writings*.

8. There are a number of reliable works on Luther's life and thought. A still reliable and helpful book is Bainton, *Here I Stand*. Also Lienhard, *Luther*.

Faith (1)

It seems that one day he was walking through a field, and a terrible lightning storm began, striking all around him. Terrified, he cried out, "St. Anne, protect me and I will become a monk!" Evidently, she did, and he did. Luther joined the monastery of Augustinian friars at Erfurt.

Young Luther's basic religion was one of fear, fear of a just and vengeful God. Luther, knowing himself to be a sinner, was continually in agony trying to appease this tyrant God. He would deny himself. He would starve himself and beat himself to keep down the flesh.

What could be behind such fear and self-loathing? Some can make a case for a kind of spiritual neurosis. But it was also the result of the teaching of the church of his day. There were many schools of thought then, but one of these had considerable influence on him.

This was the school of thought known as nominalism. The nominalists had a specific order of salvation, that is, how a sinner could become acceptable to God. We are all far from him, but he will accept us if we take the first step. The phrase they used for that step was, "Do what is in you." We may not have much good in us, but we all have some. If we make use of this, God will accept it and reward us with grace. That is, he will give us the power to do even more. If in turn we make use of this, he will give more, and we will climb higher and higher until we are in fact good enough to be acceptable to God.

This order of salvation speaks of the grace of God, even of his help to the sinner. But its very teaching can be disastrous, because it puts the burden entirely on us. Not only that, but try as we might, we never really know where we are. How far have we climbed, if at all? Am I making progress or regressing? It is no wonder that such teachings only aggravated Luther's tortured psyche.

His nominalism was to no avail. But while Luther was torturing himself with guilt and fear, his superiors eventually noticed some ability in him and sent him to study for his doctorate in Bible, which he received. He became a professor of Bible at the new university of Wittenberg. Still, doubts and fears persisted. He could not love an angry and tyrannical God.

Luther himself tells us when the breakthrough came for him. He was teaching a course on Paul's Letter to the Romans. Preparing a lecture, he came upon chapter 1, verse 17: it is often translated as, "The just shall live by faith." Perhaps a better translation might be, "The one who is just by faith shall live." It is not by my best efforts or my own righteousness that God accepts me, but by faith. I am justified before God by this faith, not by trusting in myself or my own goodness or efforts, but a faith in what God himself has done in Jesus Christ. We are called to trust in Christ, not our own piety.

Justification is by faith, not by works of the law! This revelation, gleaned from the Bible, is what has been called Luther's "Tower Experience." Now everything changed for him. He searched the entire Scripture and found evidences of this justification everywhere. Our trust is in God's grace and forgiveness, not in ourselves.

With this insight in his mind, he began to look at the church of his day to see whether its beliefs and practices conformed to it or not. Where they did not, they must be reformed! Thus was born Luther the reformer.

And there was plenty to be reformed. As previous reformers had already said, the church needed to be reformed in head and members. And that head was the papacy, desperately in need of reform. The "Renaissance popes" had survived all attempts at such reform. They basked in their power and their luxury as "vicars of Christ." They were, as has been said, "Scoundrels, but with impeccable taste"—witness the glories of the Sistine Chapel, the work of Michelangelo, financed by one of them.

The present pope, Leo X, had decided to make the Vatican, his residence, into the finest cathedral in the world. This would be extremely expensive. Where will he get the funds? He will resort to the selling of indulgences.

In that day, indulgences were seen as one way of gaining release from purgatory. It was believed that, while a perfect person could go straight to heaven, most of us needed a cleansing, or purging, before

Faith (1)

gaining access. The place for this was called purgatory. This purgatory was itself no nice place, filled with great pains to purge us of our sins. Many folk feared this place as much as hell itself.

But, according to the theory, great Christians had earned enough merits to bypass purgatory. In fact, they had earned more than they needed. These extra merits were held in what was called the treasury of saints, for use by us. Bishops and especially popes were authorized, so the theory went, to grant these to us to provide us with early release from this torture.

Pope Leo X decided that he could raise the appropriate amount of money that he needed by selling indulgences. They would be "plenary" indulgences, which granted complete freedom from the penalties of all non-mortal sins. The Holy Roman Emperor, Charles V, was also in need of money, so the two of them agreed that these indulgences would be sold in some parts of the empire, and the income was to be divided between them. At this time the archbishop of Mainz wanted to hold additional bishoprics but needed money to pay the pope to have them granted. So, he too was included.

A monk named Tetzel was given the task of making the sales. He went about parts of Germany proclaiming, "When the coin in the coffer rings, a soul from purgatory springs." We can not only buy our own freedom through this purchase, but also that of our loved ones, even those long dead.

These indulgences were not sold in Luther's actual territory, but close enough. He was enraged! He had just discovered in the Gospel that we need not purchase our salvation, even by good works, and now it was being sold for money. With this in mind, and in order to get others to respond, he sat down and wrote his Ninety-Five Theses against indulgences. He likely posted a copy of them on the chapel door at Wittenberg. The date was October 31, 1517, taken by many to be the start of the Protestant Reformation.

Every one of these theses attacked indulgences. Some were a little whimsical, such as saying that if the pope really did have this power, why did he not free all those in purgatory out of sheer Christian charity? But the main thrust clearly called into question, not only these indulgences, but much of the whole theological and ecclesiastical trimmings of the Late Middle Ages.

Reactions were swift in coming. Many sincere churchmen had been looking for a leader and decided Luther would be their man. Some would stand with him until their end. However, many would find, one by one, that they did not mean what he meant, and they would break away. The pope and his supporters, of course, were not amused.

There were various attempts to get him to retract his statements, but he would not. The pope excommunicated him. The emperor summoned him to appear before the Reichstag at Worms in 1521. Although warned against attending, he went. Appearing before them, he was ordered to recant all of his writings. His response, as it is presented to us, is historical:

> My soul is captive to the Word of God. Unless convinced by Scripture and plain reason, I cannot recant. God help me! Here I stand!

These words, "Here I stand," echoed throughout the empire, gaining new devotees to Luther. But the same words also angered both pope and emperor. Charles decreed Luther, the heretic, to be an outlaw. That is, he was now considered to be outside the protection of the law. It meant that Luther would be in danger of being punished or killed with impunity. The combined cultural forces of church and state were now arrayed against him.

Happily for him, his duke, Frederick the Wise, had him kidnapped and spirited away into the castle of the Wartburg, where he was to remain in hiding for some time, although he would continue his writing, and occasionally returned to preach from time to time. He eventually returned to Wittenberg permanently.

Luther preached many sermons and wrote volumes of theological essays and biblical commentaries. And it is during this early period that Luther wrote some works that are helpful in understanding his basic theological approach. Many of these writings are still read and felt to be helpful even today.

Faith (1)

Early on, because of his emphasis on faith, he was accused of being against the law and against good works. In defense he published a *Treatise on Good Works*. He insisted that works do become good, but only when they flow from faith, which is trusting in God and his mercy, not in our own virtues. In fact, even great works are not good unless they do so flow. Even trivial works are good if done in faith. But this faith proves itself in living, and in keeping the commandments.

In 1520 he published what to many has been his most beloved writing, *Concerting Christian Liberty*. He begins with a paradox:

> A Christian man is the most free lord of all, and subject to none; a Christian man is the most dutiful servant of all, and subject to every one.[9]

The remainder of the work is the explanation of this paradox. He presents it in terms of the inner man and the outer man. The inner man is justified and free. No outer works or situation can change this or produce Christian righteousness. Things such as vestments, offices, and fasting are of no profit here. Only one thing is necessary for life and liberty, the Gospel of Christ. We are justified by his merits alone. By no outward work is the inner man justified.

Yet we are also in the outer world, in relation to others. The believer, trusting only in God, does works to please him. Works do not justify a man, but a justified man does good works.

A parallel example: a bishop does certain things, ordains, etc., but the works do not make him a bishop. It is because he is a bishop that he does these things. So, a person is not made a Christian by doing good things but does good things because he is a Christian. We do not reject good works, he says, but only the idea that we are justified by them, rather than by the free grace of God.

Another important work of Luther: While he was in exile in the Wartburg, he responded to a challenge by a scholar named Latomus, who had objected to Luther's claim in the Ninety Five Theses that we sin even when we do good works, and even after baptism.

---

9. Luther, *Concerning Christian Liberty*.

The American Jesus?

Luther responded by again drawing the distinction between the inner and the outer man.[10] But he now coupled this with the distinction of being under the law or being in Christ. When we are under the law, we are entirely outside of Christ and under God's wrath. There is no half and half here. We are totally condemned.

But in Christ you are entirely under grace. God regards you in a new way. He does not see your sin. Instead he sees the righteousness of Christ and is positively disposed to you. Under the law, there is only God's wrath. In Christ, there is grace. Under the law, the interior man has only sin. But in Christ, God sees only our faith.

Grace is contrary to wrath; faith is contrary to sin. Grace is the way God regards you. It is not (as in Augustine) something infused. But faith is what is infused. This faith is a matter of growth. It works in us as a leaven, driving out the devil. Luther uses the example of Israel in Canaan. They possessed the land but had no final victory until David. We struggle until the final victory in Christ.

THE LATER REFORMATION

Luther's reformation spread like wildfire. Scandinavia became totally Lutheran. The English church broke away from Rome. In Zurich, Zwingli led his own reformation, in some ways differing from Luther's. The Anabaptists (wrongly titled by their opponents as "Rebaptizers") were evangelical, but were often persecuted by both Lutherans and Roman Catholics. They were never strong in Europe, but as the Baptists, they have had an immense influence in America.

Yet another powerful reformation pattern came from Switzerland in the person of John Calvin. Beginning in many ways as a Lutheran, he expanded on, and sometimes changed, Luther's teachings and practices. If anything, his influence was to be as strong as, or even stronger than, Luther's. Most of Switzerland became Calvinistic. So did the northern Netherlands. So did Scotland. In England, the Calvinistic Puritans ruled the land for a

---

10. Luther, *Against Latomus*, in Luther, *Selected Writings*, vol. 2.

Faith (1)

while. Their followers, who came to New England, would help to shape American religion and society in important ways.

With both Luther and Calvin, we encounter the knotty problem of predestination. Like Augustine, the belief in human depravity and the total need of God's grace forced them to the conclusion that our salvation can only come by the grace of God, even against our sinful wills. Calvin, if anything, stressed total reliance on God's grace even more than Luther.

But some of the groups that had at first supported Luther turned against him. One such group was the humanists, scholars who had been striving for moral reforms in the church. Erasmus was one of them. But he, like the other humanists, insisted on human free will in order to bring about the possibility of moral reforms. As he read Luther, he came more and more to the conclusion that Luther believed in predestination, not free will. Of course, he was right. He purposely baited the reformer by writing a book titled *Freedom of the Will*. Luther took the bait and responded with his own, *Bondage of the Will*, one of the strongest affirmations of predestination found anywhere. With this book, he lost the support of many of the humanists, while some still supported him.

Within Calvinism, the issue of predestination also began to take a central place. A Calvinistic scholar named Jacob Arminius was asked to study the Scriptures, defend predestination, and report to the Calvinistic Synod of Dort. Instead, he found that he could not defend it, and came out in favor of free will, a teaching known as Arminianism. Again, this doctrine will become important in America, the land of free will.

Meanwhile, the Roman Catholics were not idle. Important reforms were enacted at the Council of Trent. Anti-Protestant actions were also taken, including the approval of the Jesuits, the militant arm of the Counter-Reformation.

Soon war came in the name of the Prince of Peace. The Netherlands' War of Independence pitted Protestant against Catholic. The Huguenot wars in France did the same. In England it was Anglican against Puritan. Perhaps the most tragic of all was the Thirty Years War (1816-1848) in Germany. Political, tribal, and

The American Jesus?

religious loyalties clashed, bringing thirty years of destruction on the area, leaving Germany in shambles. It took generations for them to recover.

America is heir to all of this: differing understandings of Christian faith and life, politics mixed with faith, and more. How all of this fits with the novelties of the American experience, and whether America will be faithful to that faith or concoct something else and call it Christianity, remains to be seen.

But while Christian thinking was with some justification being questioned and rejected, another force was beginning to capture the mind of the West, often with strong anti-Christian overtones: the growing successes of human reason and science—the Enlightenment!

2

Faith (2)

MODERNITY: THE CHALLENGES TO FAITH OF MODERN SCIENCE AND PHILOSOPHY

The Enlightenment

Nature and Nature's Laws lay hid in night
God said, 'Let Newton be' And all was light.

—Alexander Pope

Crush the infamous thing

—Voltaire

No one can see his own errors;
Deliver me, LORD, from hidden faults.

—Psalm 19

Despite attempts to revive the state churches, it is no wonder that clear-headed and honest thinkers were disgusted and wanted, more than anything else, *a new start*. It is also understandable that this new start should dump the past overboard, especially the Christian past, with its rigidness, its superstitions, and its conflicting and fiercely defended doctrines, with each and

The American Jesus?

every side insisting that its was the correct way, while all were at odds with each other. It could occur to many that none of them knew the truth!

Although the new thinkers vehemently rejected the certainties of the past, they most assuredly did not reject the search for some other, more acceptable and rational certainties on which they could construct a whole system of truth. In fact, they were intent on finding a rational foundation for human knowledge. They despised many of the doctrines of Christianity but were in no way averse from holding just as strongly to their own absolutes, which, for them, were just as rational and syllogistic as those of the hated orthodox.

The dominant question was, in the midst of this intellectual chaos: are there any undeniable truths on which we can base our thoughts? It was Rene Descartes (d. 1650), the brilliant mathematician and philosopher, who set the stage for the period, and indeed for the whole Enlightenment, by offering just such a reliable (or so he though) foundation of knowledge.[1] He has been called the father of modern philosophy and may also be dubbed the father of modernity. It is difficult to find anyone in history who was as dedicated as he to starting over, which included rejecting all the ideas from the past, unless they could be proven anew.

So intent was Descartes on the new start that he prepared a room dedicated to his meditations. It was stripped of everything unessential that might remind him of the past and influence his thinking. Writing in the early decades of the seventeenth century, he began with the method of doubt. It is our duty, he insisted, to reject any and all teachings unless they are proven true. Some would suggest that we might begin with sense experience—sight, sound, etc. "No!" said Descartes. These can be mistaken, and there are disagreements among observers. This cannot give us the absolute surety that we require as a starting point. When we look into the mind, say, for geometric certainty, things seem better.

But what if God is in fact an evil demon that takes pleasure in fooling us? Since we are not sure of anything, this might be the

---

1. Decartes, *Philosophical Writings*.

Faith (2)

case. We might feel sure that one and one are two, but it may not be. We may be fooled. We still need to search for one basic truth that can serve as an axiom on which we can build an entire system. He would find just such a reliable truth!

If my mind is mistaken in its thinking, it is still thinking! This means that I exist, at least as a thinking mind. *Cogito, ergo sum.* "I think, therefore I am." It cannot be denied. I have found my foundational truth. We might notice two important things here: First, *all truth begins with me and my certainty of myself.* Second, although this was meant to be an entirely new start, Augustine, many centuries before, had already said, *Fallor, ergo sum,* "I am mistaken, therefore I am." Descartes' room and his mind were perhaps not as cleansed of the old as he imagined.

Descartes was well aware that one cannot build a mathematical system of proofs with only one truth. Therefore, he needed to look for at least one other. He knew he existed as a mind, but he also had doubts. This meant that he knew his mind to be imperfect. Thus, he had the idea of imperfection. But he could not have this idea unless he also had the idea of perfection. This idea cannot come from me, because I am imperfect. Therefore, perfection must exist to give me this idea; *therefore, perfection, or God, exists!* He had found his second truth. But note that his God is there primarily to guarantee the truth of Descartes' own system, not as any end in himself.

Descartes goes on to prove that the physical world exists, but as a reality totally different from mind. This is at the root of his well-known body/mind dualism, which has haunted the modern Western world ever since.

Being an excellent mathematician as well as a philosopher, Descartes went on to devise an entirely new mathematical system, analytic geometry, which still serves as a tool for much of modern science and engineering.

Other important thinkers were at work as well. It was during this same period when the Italian Galileo was able to demonstrate the advantages wrought by applying mathematics to careful observation, through his work on the acceleration of falling bodies. It was he too who was able to show, through the use of the telescope, the correctness of Copernicus' heliocentric hypothesis. It got him in trouble with the ecclesiastical authorities, who still insisted that the Earth was the center of the universe.

In France, especially in the last decades of the seventeenth century and into the eighteenth, there arose a group of thinkers known as "the philosophes." It was they, perhaps more than any other group, who set the stage for much of what has been taken for granted in the modern world. Disgusted with what the past had given them, they agreed with Descartes that a new start was needed, and also believed that a kind of mathematical certainty could be achieved through human reason, which was only now emerging from the ignorance and superstitions of the past, or so they thought.

Crucial to this new thinking was the growth of modern science, particularly the amazing and brilliant work of the Englishman Sir Isaac Newton. In his *Principia*, published in 1687, he was able to show that phenomena as diverse as an object falling to Earth and the planets in their orbits come under identical mechanical laws. He was also able to demonstrate that there are predictable laws governing all motion. To top this, he found that no math was available to handle his discoveries, so he invented one, the calculus. It is hard to overestimate the power of his intellect or the influence it would have on the minds of that day and on the unbelievable optimism about human reason that his discoveries engendered.

The Philosophes

A wholly new concept of the universe, of God, and of ourselves was now open. The universe is a magnificent machine, like a beautifully designed watch, running according to eternal laws. God, who is rational Mind, is the creator, who has left this perfect machine to run on its own. We too are rational, and can see the rational order of nature, as well as the moral order resident in it and in our own hearts. This view, a kind of deism, was popular among many of these philosophes. It gave them both a science and a religion to

Faith (2)

replace what they considered to be the discredited and superstitious doctrines of Christianity.

The philosophes wanted nothing less than a whole new world. As many scholars studying the period have observed, their goal was *nothing less than to transform human nature itself!* Their intentions were not only intellectual, but redemptive; to replace Christian redemption with the wholesale remaking of the human person and society, all based on reason. Here we have what Carl Becker, in his classic, *The Heavenly City of the Eighteenth Century Philosophers*, calls the seeds of much of the modern world.[2] He notes that there were four ideas that lay at the heart of their belief system, and that gave impetus to what they did. These are: that we are not depraved; that our good is found in life on Earth; that mankind, using reason alone, can perfect this good; and that we must free ourselves from ignorance and superstition, i.e., particularly from Christianity.

They would allow nothing to stand in the way of their noble task. To bring it about would require not only an entirely new idea of the universe and of God, but also a new understanding of human nature itself. Many believed that they had found just such a philosophy in deism. These new and exciting views could be found throughout Europe and in America, but France was ground zero.

Deism presented a helpful basis for all of this. God is no longer directly involved in this world. There is no need for miracles here, since the machine runs perfectly. Nor is any special revelation required, because, through reason alone, we can see the moral truth by which we can live. So God is effectively left out of the picture, at least as far as anything practical is concerned. Perhaps that is precisely where they wanted him to be: out of the picture, to let us rational folks run our own lives based on the power and beauty of our natural reason. It was Holbruch, himself an atheist, who pointed out that such a view of God might just as well lead to atheism, with no postulate of God being anymore necessary. He had a point.

---

2. Becker, *Heavenly City*.

The American Jesus?

Where does Jesus fit into all of this? *He is just like us!* A philosopher and scientist who observes the surroundings and applies reason to it! He is our teacher, a mighty good one at that; but that is all. We might well recall that Thomas Jefferson, a true son of the Enlightenment, came up with his own version of the New Testament. He clipped out all of the parts that involved either miracles or special revelations. He was left with a very small book, and with a Jesus who was nothing more than the Sage of Galilee, just as Jefferson himself was the Sage of the Potomac—a Jesus just like him. It was also a Jesus who did not need not to heal any human weakness or corruption, since no such healing was needed, thank you very much!

This Jesus will not really confront us but will simply affirm what we already are and believe. Nor does he offer forgiveness, since we really have nothing important to forgive. And spiritual healing is not necessary, since there is nothing to be healed.

Voltaire was certifiably the most influential of the philosophers of the day. A man of immense intellect and with a great spirit, he produced volumes of writings. He took humanitarian stands on such issues as the opposition to slavery. As an older man, in the years before the French Revolution, he was hailed in Paris as an almost god-like figure. In 1791, during that revolution, revolutionary leaders moved his remains to the Pantheon.

It was Voltaire who most popularized Newton in France. He also propagandized there the writings of another Englishman, John Locke. Locke, who published about the same time as Newton, was perhaps even more helpful to the philosophes than Newton had been. An empiricist, he was very different from Descartes, who had insisted that reliable knowledge could only be found within the mind. Locke, on the other hand, saw the mind as empty of content, and which could only be filled through the senses. Our minds are *tabula rasa*, blank slates, with none of Descartes "innate ideas," even though our minds do have innate operations, by which they can process what comes in.

This is exactly what the philosophes were looking for! Now at last we can see that the human mind is infinitely malleable. It can

Faith (2)

be, and has been, shaped by the content that has been thrown into it. This is the key to the human problem. We have been shaped, that is, twisted, by the errors and superstitions of the past, especially by the pernicious errors of Christianity. Now, by proper, that is, enlightened, education and by an improved political situation, our minds can be reshaped by what is rational and good and true! We can now replace grace with virtue, Scripture with nature, and Christian salvation with human perfectibility. Most of all, Locke's views free us from that dreaded and insulting doctrine of human depravity. It is likely that Locke himself saw it that way. He wrote *The Reasonableness of Christianity*, but it was a Christianity with all of the "unreasonable" parts removed.

Most of all, love for God and faith in God were replaced with love for and faith in humanity. This was really the main thrust of their agenda. Sometimes it was directed to all of humanity; sometimes it was connected with a particular human culture or nation state; but it was always an abstracted, not an empirical, humanity.

With these thoughts in mind, they were necessarily obsessed with countering any suggestion of a denial of human goodness. To them, it was just this denial that was at the heart of those Christian teachings that prevented true progress and kept humanity in the bonds of slavery and superstition. Since it has been our corrupt environment—bad education and bad political systems—that has corrupted us, we need no grace. We need only proper education and proper politics to fill the empty human mind with rational and natural truth. That is to say, *our* truth. Pelagius has been reborn, but in new dress. It never seemed to have occurred to them that human reason is itself susceptible to corruption.

There was an extreme optimism among these rationalists that is found on every page of their writings, an optimism based on their firm conviction of human perfectibility. So positive! So idealistic! So sure that human nature can now be molded in new ways that will bring about the good world that we all desire! Humanity is being freed! The future looks bright, indeed! And yet so self-righteous and so willing to question and even to deride any and all thoughts except their own presuppositions.

The American Jesus?

This helps to explain why they were so vicious in their opposition to the Christian church. They simply delighted in attacking everything about it. When Voltaire declared, "Crush the infamous thing!," it was the church that he was attacking. He was not alone. Edward Gibbon, an Enlightenment man, in his *Decline and Fall of the Roman Empire*, saw Christianity as a major element in its downfall. He concludes that it occurred because of the barbarians without and within. The barbarians within, of course, were the Christians.

Gibbon treats almost everybody with cynicism and contempt except the emperor Marcus Aurelius, who, like Gibbon, was a philosopher. Perhaps coincidentally, Marcus also persecuted Christians.

Others were happy to join in. David Hume, in his *Natural History of Religion*, was careful to connect human misery and cruelty with religious belief. Hume also insisted that no reasonable man can believe in miracles. Other writers did the same. It was common to paint Christianity in the worst light possible. A new history must now be written, opening up the possibilities of human progress and utopia, now that we are shed of the superstitions and limitations of the past. Joseph Priestly looked forward to a wonderful and glorious future. Denis Diderot, the editor of the influential *Encyclopedie*, believed that posterity would fulfill for the philosopher what heaven was to the believer. Their utter faith in human reason and basic goodness was matched by their equally total abhorrence of Christian mythology. It seems never to have occurred to most of them that they themselves might be clinging to their own myth, the myth of human rationality.

Immanuel Kant (d. 1804), a German philosopher of science, wrote *What Is Enlightenment?* He realized that we are not yet enlightened, but that man could now live according to reason and nature, not faith and miracles. The door was now open for the coming of age of humanity to a freedom from superstition.

At the same time, Kant would set limits to the depth of our knowledge, giving it some measure of humility, in his *Critique of*

Faith (2)

Pure Reason.³ He knew that all of our knowledge of reality is understood in terms of such categories as space and time. These are universal categories, applying to everything, which is why science can make judgements based on observations that are universal in nature. But if you think about it, we have never seen space or time. They are simply the way our mind sees things, the way we organize what we see. Is our world really organized this way? Perhaps it is. Perhaps not! By the nature of things, we cannot know. This can lead us to humility and pride at the same time. Humility, because we cannot know the world as it really is, but only as we see it. Pride, because we are free to calculate what we observe according to pure reason, and it will always work.

The French Revolution

Like Christianity, it was a religion of human salvation, the salvation of the world by the power of man set free by Reason.

—Christopher Dawson

The French Revolution was the laying bare of the emancipated man in his tremendous power and his terrible perversity.

—Dietrich Bonhoeffer

If we say we have no sin, we deceive ourselves ...

—First Epistle of John

A case can be made that the French Revolution brought together many of the forces at work from the Reformation to the Enlightenment, and simultaneously gave them new focus and direction.

Louis XIV, the "Sun King," had done more than anyone else to establish an absolute monarchy. Just as the sun was the center of the universe, around which all else would revolve, so he, as absolute ruler, would be both the focus and the power of all that happened in France. All areas of society and culture were subject

---

3. Kant, *Critique of Pure Reason*.

The American Jesus?

to his beneficent rule. Many of the philosophes, including Voltaire, would cling to the idea of a benevolent monarch, after the model of Plato's *Republic*. The monarch, being enlightened, could bring reason to bear on the chaos, ignorance, superstition, and injustice of the world. In fact, Voltaire had spent time with Frederick the Great with just such a hope in mind.

Louis XIV's son, Louis XV, tried mightily to reaffirm kingly absolutism, but many obstacles stood in his way. First, there was France's disastrous and humiliating defeat by the British in the French and Indian War. This, incidentally, drained the national treasury. It did not help that his own financial excesses, along with those of his mistresses, Pompadour and Du Berry, became obvious to a populace that often felt impoverished and unjustly treated. Forces were arising on all sides that dared to question the powers and privileges of the king. All these forces would have their influences when Louis XVI came to power in 1774.

As with any historical event, the French Revolution had many causes, many forces that brought it about. For one thing, Louis XVI made two strategic errors, both stemming from his support of the American Revolution. First, it has been a wise policy almost forever that one king should not support the overthrow of another, lest he encourage the same thing happening to him. It was permissible for a ruler to unseat another, but not to encourage the "rabble" to do it. But in fact, the Americans had already put into effect some of the same philosophies that were being bandied about in France. Second, that support had been expensive, further draining dry the French treasury. It was in a desperate attempt to find new sources of revenue that he bit the bullet and called the Estates General into session in May 1789. It had not met since 1614.

Many of those who were assembled had their minds filled with the heady ideas of the philosophes. They were also highly influenced by Jean-Jacques Rousseau, particularly through his work *The Social Contract* (1762).[4] He was indeed a strange and colorful man, sometimes a Roman Catholic, sometimes a Protestant. He would expose himself in his *Confessions*, a clear reference to Augustine, but only

---

4. Rousseau, *Social Contract*.

Faith (2)

exposing himself physically, as a flasher. Then again, maybe he did not. He was always controversial. At any rate, he is sometimes hailed as the founder of both romanticism and the Revolution.

Rousseau the romantic was a man of feeling. The heart rules. There is a good and pure aspect to humans, but it is not in reason; it is in the feelings. "The first impulses of our nature are always right," he insisted, because, "there is no original sin in the human heart." Thus, our own consciences can be our infallible guides, "making man like God." Perhaps he had Eden in mind here. He is at one with the philosophes in proclaiming that humans are naturally good and can even become god-like, except that he located this perfection in the heart, not the mind. Nor was he shy in proclaiming that his own heart was probably the purist of all.

In keeping with this romantic slant, he insisted that the modern technological society of his day, with its governments and sophistication, was actually corrupting—private property, science, and philosophy were included—accentuating the worst in human nature. "Man is born free," he said," yet is everywhere in chains." It must be admitted, though, that much of his railing against civilized society stemmed from his desire to find free expression for his own feelings, which were hemmed in by social mores.

Rousseau's political work, *The Social Contract*, would mark him as one of the true fathers of the revolution. In it he analyzed what a government was for, and how it ought to take shape. Locke had insisted that governments were instituted for the protection of the rights of the people; but Rousseau went further. For him, the sole purpose of government is to ensure the *welfare* of its citizens. To achieve this end, the people themselves, not the king, are the real sovereign. They determine the policies of the elected government by majority vote. Each person, and the government itself, must obey these policies, because each will have bound himself to the "general will," one of his chief ideas. By contract, each individual agrees to abide by this will, whatever it may be, even against his perceived self-interest. Thus, they are free because they have freely chosen to follow that general will. By such a reorientation in government, human nature itself could be changed. He saw problems with humankind, but they did not belong as much to man as to man badly governed.

There is more here than a hint of revolution. The thinkers of the Enlightenment had often looked to an enlightened monarch to bring their ideas to fruition. They looked to such rulers as Catherine II and Frederick II for their dream to become realized. Not Rousseau!

Much of Rousseau seems somewhat tame to our modern ears, but it was exhilarating for many who had been reared in a world of nobles and kings, ruling by divine right. It gave them a way in which government can be the instrument for the improvement of mankind. In this sense, he can be called a man of the revolution. The philosophes sought reform. Rousseau had given the formula for revolution. This was "just what the doctor ordered" for those who were to become its leaders. With Rousseau there was a shift in understanding who the real enemy was. With the philosophes, it had been religion and the church. These were still considered as enemies, but now the sharpest criticisms would be leveled against the state.

To return to the Estates General: The assembly had three units or sections, or "estates": the nobles, the clergy, and the commoners, each with its own collective vote. It should not be thought that the "commoners" were poor folk, representing the dispossessed of society. Most of them were actually fairly prosperous lawyers or businessmen, who often felt that their considerable contributions to the new economy were not being appropriately recognized or rewarded. They resented the nobles, who had played important parts in society in years gone by but who still insisted on the old-time privileges, even though their importance had seriously diminished.

All of this and more was in play when the meeting took place. The beliefs, the hopes, and the dreams of Rousseau and the philosophes had been at work in France, especially among the elites, and those who would become the leaders of the revolution were enamored with just such ideas.

Things moved swiftly. An angry crowd gathered before the hated prison, the Bastille. When the army joined in on the side

Faith (2)

of the crowd, the Bastille was stormed and its director was killed. July 14, 1789, Bastille Day, is still celebrated as the beginning of the revolution.

In August, the National Assembly, a union of the three "estates," did away with the feudal system and its privileges. More important, it would pass its famous Declaration of the Rights of Man. This idealistic and powerful document, along with the slogan, "Liberty, Equality, Fraternity," would now serve as the energizing force not only of the revolution but also for generations to come. It guaranteed liberty and stated that that every man would have no limits to the exercise of these rights. Persons are to be presumed innocent; only such acts as are injurious to the public good may be punished, etc.

The church was not exempt from assembly action. By November, church property was expropriated. In 1790, the Civil Constitution of the Clergy was adopted. All clergy must swear allegiance to the state. The pope condemned this, and many clergy refused to swear. Priests who refused to swear were forbidden to practice their ministry. A division arose within France, with many of the faithful, especially in rural areas, supporting the non-jurors.

The first outbreak of serious violence occurred in Paris, the "September Massacres." Things had not been going well. An alliance of foreign powers was invading; there was lack of food; there was little effective government to bring order. The first attack of the people centered on non-juring priests, with more than 100 of them being killed. By the time it was over, nearly 1,400 prisoners, "enemies of the republic," had been slain. It was a harbinger of things to come. By December, the king was put on trial, with many calling for his head. He was executed in January 1793.

Also in that January, a "Committee on Public Safety" was instituted. By April, Maximilian Robespierre became its most influential member. In September, the "Reign of Terror" began. Many "traitors" were guillotined. Robespierre would call for both virtue and terror to ensure the success of the revolution. By the time it was over, thousands died in Paris, and many more outside

The American Jesus?

it, especially Catholics throughout the countryside. Terror and intimidation were everywhere in order to ensure the rights of man.

Meanwhile, there was a religious division within the leadership. The atheists, in the tradition of Voltaire and others, insisted that only reason should rule, with all religion eschewed. Robespierre and those affiliated with him wanted religion, but it would be deism, not Christianity. In fact, both groups keenly desired the eradication of the Christian faith.

Each held ceremonies as professions of their respective faiths. In November of 1793 the atheists held a "Festival of Reason" in Notre Dame, now dubbed a "temple of reason." A young woman posed as the representative of reason. During the same period, the churches in Paris were closed.

In June 1794, Robespierre countered with his own "Festival of the Supreme Being." Robespierre himself came forth with a bouquet in one hand and a torch in the other, inaugurating the new religion of humanity that would purge the world of ignorance, vice, and folly.

Ironically, this festival was held during the height of the Reign of Terror, in which period more than 1,440 persons were being executed in Paris alone! If it was possible for Christians to go to war, killing others in the name of the Prince of Peace, it was also possible for persons to commit wholesale slaughter in the name of humanity, reason, and the purity of the human heart.

In July it was all over with the overthrow and quick execution of Robespierre himself. But not quite over! Shortly afterward, 80 of his followers were put to death. But with the new Directorate, cooler heads would come to prevail.

Yet, despite these horrors, true believers in reason still clung to the natural goodness and purity of humanity, qualities that could be released by proper education and the abandonment of Christian superstition. Carl Becker points out that, for these rationalists, if the regenerated, perfected humanity could not come in their generation, it would certainly come about in the future. It would be their this-worldly and humanistic "heavenly city." Utopia was still possible, but on strictly human grounds. No need for grace here.

Faith (2)

Condorcet, a leading Enlightenment thinker, while proscribed and in hiding from the terror, finds consolation in the future perfectibility of humanity! Such faith! And despite the empirical evidence, that humanistic faith would continue into the centuries that followed and form an important basis of the modern world.

As for the revolution itself, it was eventually taken over by Napoleon, whose great victories enabled him to lead the revolution, and in its name to spread humanism and brotherly love throughout Europe in the bloodiest possible fashion. He was portrayed by many as a romantic, historic figure. Eventually he made himself emperor, symbolically taking the crown from the pope and crowning himself.

The failures and horrors of the French Revolution sent shock waves through the modern world, yet true believers still believed in, and some continue to believe in, reason.

America

In America, the battle between traditional Christianity and the modern world of the new science and philosophies came to a head, as it had in Europe, not only for intellectuals, but for the common people. It was Charles Darwin's theory of evolution, especially when applied to the human race, that had the greatest impact, with believers on one side and the devotees of the new science on the other.

"Some call it evolution, others call it God" (William Carruth). Belief in the traditional understandings of biblical accounts, such as the creation story, were now held up to question, and even ridicule, as never before. Those who were already disposed to attack Christianity now found new ammunition for their attacks.

A second area where science caused grief for many believers was in biblical studies. There had always been questions about the veracity of scriptural accounts. But now, coming mostly from Germany, and from other places as well, a flood of studies attempted to apply textual and critical methods to Scripture itself. They presented a whole new way of looking at the Bible and generated the

The American Jesus?

most severe kinds of challenges to what had almost always been considered as "biblical truths."

Other Christians reacted in the opposite direction, basically rejecting the modern world or at least major aspects of it. Among these were the Fundamentalists, who felt the need to defend scriptural truth against the onslaught of biblical criticism. In 1910 they articulated their *five fundamentals*, which they considered to be absolutely necessary to preserve the traditional faith. First of these was "the verbal inerrancy of Scripture," clearly indicating that attacks on Scripture were their major concern. Evidently, suggestions were made that the teaching of grace be included within these fundamentals. This was rejected. Clearly, the attack on the Bible, not the need for this grace, was paramount.

The issues of literal scriptural truth in conflict with evolutionary philosophy came to a head in 1925 at the Scopes Trial, or so-called Monkey Trial in Dayton, Tennessee. Scopes was accused of teaching evolution in public school. William Jennings Brian, who had earlier run for president, became the prosecutor. Clarence Darrow, a liberal defense lawyer, rushed to the defense. The trial became a cause célèbre in the nation, and most found it to be an embarrassment and a setback for the Fundamentalist cause. Fundamentalism was a rearguard action at best, yet it is still an important element in American Protestant thought, although its adherents are now usually referred to as Evangelicals rather than Fundamentalists. In defense of these Fundamentalists, it must be noted that Bryan and others were also opposed to evolution on social and moral grounds, because of its detrimental effect on human welfare and its tendency to degrade the status of humans, seeing us as mere animals.

This debate about evolution did not long remain among the intellectuals, but quickly "trickled down" to the common man. Will Rogers joked that he had a hard time believing in the story of the flood, because he couldn't see how all of these animals could stay together in one place with the skunk.

At about the same time, Enlightenment influences were being felt within the church itself, in the form of Unitarianism. Even

Faith (2)

Calvinist New England was influenced by the American concept of free will and personal responsibility, as well as by the new intellectual forces. By the early nineteenth century, Unitarianism became a dominant religious force in that area. In 1819, William Ellery Channing, one of its leaders, delivered his address on what that group believed and stood for.[5]

As one would expect, he addressed the Unitarian rejection of the Trinity and of the two natures of Jesus Christ. But he devoted a great deal of his presentation to his clear abhorrence of the idea of the irresistible will of God. He deeply resented such a tyrannical, and he would say, immoral deity. In its place he conceived of a God who is truly just and regards the moral worth of virtue. Such a good God would never bring us into the world morally depraved. So he felt!

Jesus himself came into the world, said Channing, not to pay some price, but to effect a moral or spiritual deliverance of mankind: to engender knowledge, love, and obedience to our creator. It is impossible not to see the moral earnestness of Channing. God is moral, not tyrannical. And we are at root morally responsible beings.

In America, we are still dealing with the tensions between the need for grace and our "can do" spirit, which insists that we are perfectly capable of making all the necessary decisions completely on our own, thank you very much!

It is interesting that, by the time of the American Revolution, Methodism had become America's largest denomination. It somehow appealed to the American spirit. John Wesley was, of course, one of its major influences. He insisted on our ability to respond to God's call. Any idea of our inability to do so was anathema to him. He wrote *Predestination Calmly Considered*. His presentation was in fact hardly calm at all. He deeply resented it. It went against everything that he was trying to do. And it is no accident that his brand of Christianity prospered well in this free-will country, opposing, as it does, any affirmation of grace that might deny our own ability to choose God.

---

5. Channing, "Unitarian Christianity."

CHRISTIANITY AND (POST)MODERNISM

...as if a man fled from a lion,
And a bear met him...

—Amos 5:19

"The more things change, the more they stay the same." During the past few centuries, the Christian community has struggled to reorient itself and understand its message in terms of the modern age and culture—the culture in which we have little choice but to live and have our being. In this struggle we are, in our own way, re-enacting what our forebears experienced over the centuries, although each age has had its form of the battle.

The United States is likely the most modern of nations. While it is true that much of what we have comes from Europe—human rights, Christianity, philosophies, and political structures—the American experience has shaped and reshaped them into something new. Individualism, capitalism, positive thinking, and denominationalism are all part of this combination.

We have accepted various forms of Christianity, while being able, to some extent, to merge them together into the going concern called America. Even the nations and peoples that supplied us with the elements of success in the modern world often stand in somewhat resentful awe at our success. Various forms of accommodation have been tried here, each one with its own partial successes and partial failures in holding on to the faith, while also being loyal to our cultural surroundings. We have found that modernity must be reckoned with, like it or not.

And yet, the very successes and accomplishments of modernity have raised important issues that might force us to question the most basic beliefs of the modern views of life, the very beliefs that we have struggled to relate to. A whole new cultural set of beliefs and values has raised its head to replace the very modernism that has been such an important aspect of our lives and beliefs. It is called postmodernism!

Faith (2)

Postmodernism is a view of life that finds itself wondering about, not just this or that about the modern enterprise, but its very basis. Very few will question the great benefits of the modern world, especially in the hard sciences and engineering. But serious issues are being raised about its sufficiency as a philosophy that we can still use, and on which we can base society and our individual lives. Postmodernists insist that there are important aspects of human life that are either left untreated by modernism, or denied by it. And some of these issues are important and even central to human life. Some examples are social issues, matters of justice, aesthetics, personal ethics, and self-understanding. Attempts to apply the accepted scientific methods to these areas have often seemed forced and are less than helpful.

A number of postmodern thinkers refer to the beliefs of the modern world, beginning with Descartes and then Kant, as "foundationalism," where a firm foundation is given, or at least, thought to be given, to our knowledge and understanding. It is precisely this foundation that has now been ripped away from us.

All of us, it is said, are in our own cultural box, and all of our understanding takes place within that box. There is no way out! They insist on this. Now a kind of total relativism begins to raise its head. For many postfoundationalists the heart of our problem is with language. We think in terms of our own language. Someone of a different language system will necessarily think differently than we do. There is truly no way out of this. If there is truth to this view, then our cultures may well influence us in crucial ways that we cannot transcend, nor overcome.

A clear implication of this approach is that it can lead to atheism, even nihilism, including a rejection of the Christian faith. This is in fact the case with one of the most important European thinkers, Friedrich Nietzsche (d. 1900), who for some is a kind of "patron saint" of postmodernism. "God is dead!" he said.

Nietzsche, profound, exciting, and certifiably insane, is one of the prophets of postmodernism. His keen intellect and troubled soul realized, before most did, that the certainty of the belief

The American Jesus?

systems of modernity was no longer viable, and we are left with nothing! Nihil!

One of the most well-known presentations of Nietzsche's views is a parable in his "Joyful Wisdom."[6] In this parable, the madman (evidently Nietzsche himself) comes into the marketplace crying, "I seek God! I seek God!." The cynics there laugh at him, asking such question as, "Is he lost?" or "Did he emigrate?" But the madman is deeper than they are. He persists: "I tell you where God is. We have killed him."

Nietzsche knew very well the terrible implication of this murder. "What were we doing when we unchained this earth from its sun? Whether is it moving now? . . . Are we not plunging continually? . . . God is dead. God remains dead and we have killed him . . ." Nietzsche was clearly ahead of his time. But that time has come. If not with virulent atheism, at least with a world where God is absent—an atheism in practice. It must be asked whether this is the case with many Americans. Where for many, our Earth is truly unhinged from its sun and plunging. Plunging to where we do not know, without our being aware of what is happening. What are the ways that Christians can respond to this, if there are any?

It seems we are caught in an intellectual bind. On the one hand, we have struggled to adapt ourselves to the blessings and threats of modernity and with some, although partial, success. Now, at the same time, postmodernism raises its head, attacking our beliefs from the opposite direction. Now the question is no longer how we can confront a very self-confident belief system that opposes our faith, but a view that questions any and all beliefs, including those of that modernism that we have tried so hard to confront. Some of us feel beset on both sides, still dealing with the challenges of the modern world, while trying to face its opposite at the same time.

A number of present-day thinkers simply refuse to face these difficult issues and merely go about their business, content with being continual seekers with no real belief that they can find any worthwhile answers these troubling questions.

---

6. Kaufmann, *Nietzsche*, 96–97.

Faith (2)

But one possible way to respond is to point out that many of the postmodernists themselves are living in a self-contradiction. If all statements are relativized and not intimately related to reality, would this not also apply to this statement itself? The denial of all truths certainly must also apply to the truth of that denial. What foundation is there for denying foundations?

Yet some postmoderns have found a more positive answer to the destructiveness of their own wrecking ball. Since all truths are being reduced to some kind of subjective faith rather than knowledge of reality, this leaves the door open, or at least ajar, for faith itself, and thus for Christianity to compete on an equal level, since what have been thought to be absolute truths, philosophical, psychological, and scientific, are now exposed to be faiths themselves.

Not only Christian beliefs, but the certainties of the Enlightenment, the French Revolution, Marxism, scientism, and the rest, which have been used as a weapon to attack the faith, are now open to be bitten by the same dog. At any rate, the door is now open for some honest discussion with the gods of our own culture on an equal basis.

Neither of these answers is truly convincing. Yet we continue to struggle, as others have, to understand our faith within the parameters of the world as we think we know it. We can take some comfort that our situation is not new. The earliest Christians had to struggle with their relation to their Jewish heritage and then to a hostile Roman culture. Then the question of being the political ruling class was thrust upon them. Then the struggles of the Middle Ages were their lot. This was followed by the various permutations of modernity.

Now, following in that long train of Christian believers, ever struggling to come to terms with their world and its beliefs, and how to relate to it, we must begin to see that we face issues that have been paralleled throughout history. And we can take comfort that we can learn from their faith and their efforts, although at the present time we may see through a glass darkly.

3

Hope

We have met the enemy, and he is us.

—Pogo

When faced with evils, we place the cause of them either in the individual human heart and society or in natural causation. We might call the first evil, our own, the ones we commit, "moral evil"; the second, "natural evil." Both are painful. An appropriate cure should deal with one or the other. The Bible deals with both. Moral evil, or sin, must be recognized and admitted. It can only be handled by repentance and forgiveness. Natural evil may be seen either as the work of a malignant or angry being or simply as the way things are in this uncertain world.

    It is difficult to find anything in human experience that is more disheartening and disorienting than this problem of evil. It is part of the lives of all of us: children die of cancer, older folks suffer from dementia, human relations fall apart with great pain. Failures hurt. And added to all is this, there are the troubles and difficulties that come with simply living in this world; whole populations are subjected to famines, wars, dictators, diseases, climate changes, and more.

Hope

Even the deservedly praised accomplishments of science, we find, can just as easily be used to cause human misery, slavery, and chaos, despite the nobler efforts of humanity. Witness the uses of technology by the Nazis, and the successful application of weapons of mass destruction to whole populations.

It does not seem right! Anyone with even the most minimal sense of decency will be outraged and shake his fist at the heavens over these things, wondering whether we have any reason to hope.

Why must this be? And where is God in all this? Many folks who take these things seriously and have a conscience, reject any God or at least any good God, after the outrageous atrocities of Hitler and his henchmen, or of Stalin and his party. Many have lost their faith over just this issue. Others maintain their faith but turn their backs on the problem and simply go about their business as best they can. But the fact of evil still creeps into all of our psyches, like it or not.

On top of this, most of us are well aware of the possibilities, and even the fact, that evil dwells in our own souls. It is there in what we do, and in what we do not do, and in what we would really like to do, admit it or not. Psychiatrists do a lot of business trying to salve our troubled consciences.

As often as not, we are faced with placing our hope in ourselves, or in some natural processes, or in God. The problem, and the myriad of approaches to it, can be seen throughout the course of history, as a review of them will show.

Yet today we are in a particular spot. As modern men and women, we can rejoice in all the advantages that our world offers us, in science, medicine, and the arts. But we still find ourselves continually looking over our shoulders to see what evil is prepared to strike.

As American Christians, we are in a kind of double bind over these things. How can we Americans, with our innate optimism, face these disheartening facts of life? To make matters worse, how can we, worshipers of the Father of our Lord Jesus Christ, explain these evils to others, or even to ourselves? To start, we must face them, without trying to explain them away. There is no Pollyanna denial of human pain and suffering here. Yet Christians also proclaim a Christian hope in spite of it all.

THE FACT OF EVIL IN THE SCRIPTURES

It has been said that all, or at least most, of the Old Testament is an attempt to justify God to humans in the face of evil. But we do know that at least the Scripture does take the problem seriously.

To begin with, Scripture strongly affirms that God is good and that his world is good. In the creation story in Genesis, as the days of creation roll on, God looks at his works and, one by one, he proclaims, "It was good,'" and again, "It was good." Again and again, the goodness of the created world is affirmed.

Yet evil, it says, came into the world through the serpent. It is important that the temptation he offers to the human pair is simply," You will be like God." Rather than being content to be happy and good creatures, the temptation is to be divine (Genesis 1–3).

Here we see several things: First, it is affirms that there really is some evil force in the world, whether we like to admit it or not. And in fact, by not admitting its existence, we might become greater prey to its effects. Second, humans, on our own responsibility, do cooperate with this force, often to our ruin. Third, our weakness is often, in our own minds, our strength. In their pride, Adam and Eve thought of themselves as more than they were and disobeyed their creator. By attempting to climb up, they fell.

Some of the prophets, too, relate human suffering to our own misbehavior. For example, Amos, in the midst of a famine, tells the people that God gave them "cleanness of teeth," i.e., poverty, because of their own disobedience.

Of course, there is more to evil and suffering than simple human disobedience. There are terrible tragedies that are larger than human errors. Nowhere is this presented more clearly and more forcefully than in the book of Job, where we find a somewhat different approach to the difficult problem of evil and suffering.

First, it is clear that Job is a good man, so his suffering cannot be a just punishment for his sins. His servants were killed; there

Hope

was also fire from heaven; his sons and daughters were slain; he was afflicted with terrible, painful sores, and ended up sitting on a pile of ashes in suffering. He was advised to curse God and die. But he would not.

Time after time he cried out in pain, questioning God. His "friends" insisted that since God is just, his pains must be his own fault.

Yet Job appeals to God for some answer. The answer he gets seems hardly satisfying. God tells him that he, God, will question Job, not the other way around. God asks, "Where were you when I laid the foundations of the world?" "Or," God adds, "made the clouds? Or the snow, or the hail, or made the crocodile, and so on? Even if I told you, you would not understand!" Job, like Adam, must face his own non-divinity!

It is important to realize that in much of the Bible the approach to the problems of suffering and evil is not to understand their origins, *but to figure out how to deal with them*! This is true of both testaments, both Old and New.

In the New Testament, the Greek word for "hope," *elpis*, is not found in the Gospels at all, and the verb for "to hope," *elpizo*, very rarely. But they are both found in abundance in the remainder of the New Testament.

And the concept is almost everywhere present, even in the Gospels, especially in relation to Jesus himself. He heals those with hopeless diseases. He offers forgiveness to those overcome with despair over guilt.

He himself, of course, is in constant combat with demonic forces of evil. In the Gospel of Matthew he begins his ministry by being tempted in every way possible, yet emerges victorious. At another time, when he is accused of casting out demons by the power of the prince of demons, he tells his critics that a strong man rules over his goods until one stronger than he emerges to cast him off. The message is clear: he is the stronger one who casts off the demonic ruler over humanity.

But it is in his own life that he feels the powers of evil everywhere. The Jewish leaders mock him. The crowds who had followed him, and even his own disciples, desert him. The combined cultural and religious powers team up to falsely accuse him, and sentence him to death. He feels, on the cross, that even his heavenly Father deserts him. He dies.

But in the midst of all this, he rises from the dead! He is victorious over all of the forces that have been arrayed against him. There is hope, even in the midst of life's worst sins and tragedies. And this hope is also for the rejected, the outcast, and the sinner. We now can have such a hope, based not on a Pollyanna kind of optimism, but on faith in him.

The one most often proclaiming hope is Paul. And for him it is almost always connected with Jesus Christ and his resurrection. According to Acts, when Paul is on trial before the council, he says, "I am on trial concerning the hope of the resurrection of the dead." In his writings we again see this insistence on hope being central to the Christian life. He desires that the Romans "abound in hope." And, "In hope we were saved." And again, "If for this life only we have hoped in Christ, we are of all people most to be pitied, but in fact Christ has been raised from the dead, the first fruits of those who have died" (1 Cor 15:19-20).

Paul had himself experienced suffering of many kinds because of his faith, yet he clung to that faith as the basis of his hope. He says in Romans 8, "I consider that the sufferings of this present time are as nothing compared to the glory to be revealed to us . . . If God is for us, who is against us? Who will separate us from the love of Christ? Will hardship or distress, or persecution, or famine or nakedness, or peril, or sword? . . . No, in all these things we are more than conquerors through him who loved us."

THE HOPE OF ULTIMATE VICTORY

The claim of something finite to infinity or to divine greatness is the characteristic of the demonic.

—PAUL TILLICH

Hope

Gnosticism[1]

Gnosticism was an early attempt to deal with the problem of evil in such a way that we can not only face it, but also overcome its powers over us. It saw the divine Jesus as the way to return to escape these evils and find our true place in the cosmos.

Gnosticism was a religious/philosophical system that was quite popular and influential, particularly in the second Christian century. Yet, there were so many differing schools of the movement, some Christian, some not, that it is hard to generalize about them. But there are some characteristics that are common to most of them.

One of these characteristics is that they were extreme dualists. They saw the world in terms of the contrast and antagonism between spirit and flesh, good and evil. These two are in a cosmic battle, infecting the whole universe. This battle also exists within the human person, where our minds are dragged down by the weight and lowliness of our physical bodies.

It is also a religion of salvation, which, for them, amounted to the escape of the good soul from the evil body. This is accomplished by our coming to realize our situation through knowledge, or *gnosis*. This self-awareness of our dual nature was central to them.

Plato's "Know thyself" could have been their slogan. Know that the source of your pain is your inner tensions and contradictions! Know also that your salvation, the way out, is through knowledge, knowledge of your true situation!

Whenever we experience evils, we ask about God. If God does the evil, he is evil. Some have felt that way today because of Nazism, and other woes. If God is incapable of stopping what is wrong, he is weak and need not be worshipped. The third option is the one taken by the Gnostics: God is totally above and unconnected to these evils.

How then do we account for the sorry state of this world? *Their God* is totally beyond the world, they say, separated from it and unknowable. He has nothing to do with creation. The Gnostics

---

1. See Rudolph, *Gnosis*.

conceive of reality as an emanation or flow down from this God, step by step through many realities, and from unity to more and more multiplicity, as a champagne fountain flows down from one level to another. Because of this emanation, each level, from the highest to the lowest, still has something of the divine in it, though, of course, much less for the lower levels.

The Gnostics have elaborate names for each of these levels: church, Christ, etc. But it must be remembered that these realities have little to do with those beings that we think are indicated by these names. Instead, they locate spiritual realities in what they call the *pleroma*, the spiritual realms, each having symbolic significance.

Each level of this reality descends lower and lower, farther and farther from the highest reality. Near the bottom is a being named, following Plato, the *demiurge*. This being is low, but still has something of the divine in it, as all realities do. This is the one who is responsible for creation, and it explains why our world is so full of pain and chaos.

We are the result of this declension. We are part of this evil and painful physical world, but we do have the divine within us! Our salvation is to know this and climb back higher and higher to be at one with our true spiritual self.

This odyssey, this fall and restoration, like everything else, is expressed in mythical terms.

One example for those who were in the Jewish/Christian Gnostic tradition, is the treatment of the story of creation and fall. For them, it is not the high God who put us into this created world, but the demiurge. The serpent is not the devil, but a representative of the higher, spiritual world. By telling them to eat of the tree of knowledge, he is inviting them to gnosis and spiritual awakening so they may escape from the garden of the demiurge. When they do eat, they come to realize their true, spiritual nature. It is the evil creator who then punishes them.

The Gnostics believed that Jesus is the Savior, because he comes from the higher world to teach us our unity with God and the way back to him. Yet as our Savior, he must be fully spiritual,

Hope

and have no truck with the physical world. He only *appears to be fully human*. He could not really be born, or suffer, or die. In one account of the crucifixion, Jesus uses his powers to cloud men's minds so that he appears to be Simon of Cyrene, and Simon appears to be Jesus, so poor Simon is crucified, not Jesus.

The ethics of the Gnostics was fully consistent with their philosophy. In theory, at least, they would abstain from sex. Of course, most of them did not. One of the Gnostic groups reversed this and tried to show their contempt for the limits of creation by taking advantage of it by the extreme use of it, eating and sex and in other ways. Some of today's sophisticated Gnostics may be of the same mind.

It is clear that if some of them were Christians, they had a Christianity that denied some of what most Christians deem to be the basics of their faith. The Gnostics could not believe that God is the creator of this world, or that the creation is good. Nor, as we have seen, were they able to think that Jesus was a real flesh-and-blood man who was born, hungered, suffered, and died. Gnosticism was a noble effort to fit Jesus into the best philosophies of the day to make him understandable and acceptable to his culture. Again, some of this same effort is still with us today.

Irenaeus and the Gnostics

Irenaeus was bishop of Lyon in what is now southern France, during the second century. He became bishop there upon the martyrdom of the previous bishop. It is possible that Irenaeus himself was eventually martyred. He was among those who used their pens to oppose the teachings of the Gnostics. His massive work *Against Heresies* is one of the classics of the early church fathers. In it he deals with many forms of what he conceived to be harmful errors, but Gnosticism takes central place.[2]

He opposed the Gnostic otherworldly, speculative knowledge with his own gnosis, which is far less speculative, and deeply rooted

---

2. Irenaeus, *Against Heresies*.

in Scripture. He also insisted that his theology was in succession from the apostles. He said that he had personally met Polycarp, who had known the apostle John.

Irenaeus sees the creation and the human situation in dramatic terms. So, one way of approaching his ideas can be in terms of a dramatic unfolding, having a beginning, a middle, and an end.

A second way of understanding him can be seen in terms of two basic terms: the *oikoumene*, or "arrangement," how God arranges things in a way that is always sufficient for a positive outcome. The second is the *recapitulation*, or "re-heading," of humanity in Jesus Christ, our new and proper head, who sets things right where Adam did them wrong.

The Beginning: Creation

For Irenaeus, there is only one God, and that God is good! He, the high God, not some lower demiurge, is the creator; so the creation is good, not an evil prison house for the soul. It is a gift.

There is also a total distinction between God and his creation, between God and humanity. Even where there is a closer and closer relation to him, the distinction of creator/ creature always remains. So nowhere is there any idea of our gradually realizing our imagined divinity. No deification here![3]

God created humans for happiness, that is, for eternal life with him. As such, we are created in the "image" and the "similitude" of God. The *image* of God, for Irenaeus, is that we have rationality and a free will. These are never lost, so we are always morally responsible. But the *similitude* is that we are made to grow more and more to be like God, by trusting in him. Irenaeus believed that we were created in an immature state, needing to "grow up" spiritually to be more and more like God. He grants us his Spirit to enable us to grow. But by turning from God, we lose this help, this Spirit, and destine ourselves to a state of perpetual spiritual immaturity.[4]

---

3. Irenaeus, *Against Heresies* 4.11.2; 4.38.1.
4. Irenaeus, *Against Heresies* 5.16.2; 5.6.1.

Hope

The Middle: The Fall

The serpent, whom Irenaeus equates with the devil, sees that humans are destined to become the highest in creation, higher than himself. So, out of jealousy, he tempts them to turn away from God. Note that the devil, in Gnostic thinking, represents the better, higher reality, but is here seen by Irenaeus as the opposite, the bringer of ruin.

And ruin it was. By following the temptations and deceits of Satan, and turning from God, humans lose his Spirit, fall into decay and death. They become captives of Satan, without the strength to escape. So they will be perpetual children, never able to grow up spiritually. And they will bring unmitigated tragedy upon themselves.

The End: Victory

Yet God has arranged his creation in such a way that he is sufficient to cope with this disruption of it. He does this through the recapitulation, or re-heading, of humanity. Adam, the head of humanity, did it wrong, and brought tragedy upon the race. God sends us Jesus Christ, the second Adam, the new head, who sets things right.

Jesus is both God and human. With the power of God, he resists Satan, and thus frees humanity from his grasps. But to do this, as a human, he must grow through every stage of human life, from childhood on.

In the incarnation, he recapitulates the battle that we have fought and lost, and on our behalf, as a human with God's power, he wins! After his baptism, his first act is to go into the desert, and there he is tempted by the devil. He is hungry and tempted in almost every possible way, but he resists. He wins! Jesus reverses the situation. Humanity, in the person of Adam, in the garden fell. The human Jesus in the desert wins.[5]

---

5. Irenaeus, *Against Heresies* 4.11.2.

The American Jesus?

Later, when his opponents claim that he casts out demons by the power of the prince of demons, he tells them that if a strong man holds others captive, they cannot escape until a stronger comes along to unseat him and free them. Clearly, he is referring to himself and his victorious battle as a human against Satan.

The conqueror is conquered. Eden is reversed. Humanity now has a new head. Eve's disobedience is reversed by Mary's obedience. Adam's eating the forbidden fruit is overcome by Jesus' fasting. The tree of Eden is reversed by the tree of Calvary.[6]

It is essential for Irenaeus that the one who wins this battle must be truly human, since it is humans who are so enslaved. Any suggestion that he is not really a human, as with the Gnostics, is thrown out. He is enfleshed and must be born and hunger and die. Yet he must also be divine, so he can defeat evil with the power of God.[7]

We have noted that Irenaeus is his own kind of Gnostic. He believes that knowledge is essential to salvation. The incarnation is revelation. By defeating our enemies, Jesus shows us what God is like, what being a true man is like, and what a human in union with God can do. Seeing these things, we are now open to the Spirit again, and begin to again grow up spiritually.

What we see about God is his graciousness. We learn that he is the source of our deliverance. We experience forgiveness and come to love God more.

Thus, our similitude is restored. We can become imitators of Christ, grow in our fellowship with God, progress morally, and grow in ethical uprightness.

Our hope for ourselves and for the human race is to know both our own state and the graciousness of God.[8]

After Irenaeus, Gnosticism began losing its influence. But it, and the questions it raised, have persisted in one form or other until today. The first form of it concerns the nature of evil. The

---

6. Irenaeus, *Against Heresies* 4.11.2.
7. Irenaeus, *Against Heresies* 4.38.2.
8. Irenaeus, *Against Heresies* 3.5.3; 3.20.2; 5.8.2; 5.9.4.

Hope

second regards human nature itself, and whether we possess an inner self, which is akin to the divine, God within us.

First, in the Bible, and especially in the teachings of Jesus, we see that evil forces are personalized as demons and as the devil himself. This view has persisted through the years, with various ways of approaching it. Some of the gargoyles on medieval cathedrals are portrayals of demons, hoping that we can reduce their power over us.

This belief in demonic forces is represented in no less a person than Martin Luther. We know the legend that the devil was so real to him that he threw an ink well at him. In 1961 Gustaf Aulen wrote *Christus Victor*, where he showed that Luther's theology was in the tradition of Irenaeus, that life is a battle against evil forces, but we have the hope of victory through Jesus Christ.[9] A look at Luther's most famous hymn, "A Mighty Fortress,"[10] lends credence to Aulen's idea:

> A mighty fortress is our God,
> A sword and shield victorious:
> He breaks the cruel oppressor's rod
> and wins salvation glorious.
> The old satanic foe,
> Has sworn to work us woe!
> with dread craft and might he arms himself to fight.
> On earth he has no equal.
> No strength of ours can match his might!
> We would be lost, rejected.
> But now a champion comes to fight,
> Whom God himself elected.
> Ask who this may be? The Lord of hosts is he!
> Christ Jesus mighty Lord, God's only Son adored.
> He holds the field victorious.

Clearly, Luther had no trouble conceiving of evil in a personalized form, but more important, he also conceived of our hope as personal in Jesus Christ. As modern persons, we may not find such

---

9. Aulen, *Christus Victor*.
10. In *Lutheran Book of Worship*, #229.

The American Jesus?

a belief to be credible. We are amused by pictures of Satan having horns and a tail and wearing red underwear. Perhaps we are also amused by Flip Wilson, as Rev. Leroy's wife, who said that "The devil made me buy this dress!"

But it is hard to deny that there seems to be some kind of evil force afoot in our world. Witness the all too common situations where individuals and even mass movements seem to be controlled by suprahuman forces: Hitler, Pol Pot, world-wide Stalinism, mass shootings and more. There are all kinds of attempts to explain these things in terms of individual or mass psychology. Perhaps some commentators have been right in saying that the devil has much more influence over us when we refuse to admit that he exists.

But probably a much more difficult attack on Christian thinking is the continuance of Gnosticism. Actually, in the Middle Ages, a few groups continued Gnostic beliefs in some form or other.

AMERICAN GNOSTICISM?

There are clearly American versions of Gnosticism. In the late 1800s, Edward Bellamy published *Looking Backward*,[11] expressing a utopian dream of his day—and of people in many ages. In it, the hero, Julian West, had been one of the idle rich, living in luxury, oblivious to the Dickensian poverty, misery, and degradation that surrounded him in Boston. But by a strange set of circumstances, he went to sleep in 1887, only to awake in the year 2000.

He found the world immensely changed, in all aspects for the better. A totally new society had emerged. Prosperity is everywhere and for all. Greed and injustice have been done away. The arts and sciences flourish. Morality is improved. Slums and unhealthy conditions are nowhere to be found. There is a world in peace.

How did this all come about? The answer is as simple as it is obvious: a benevolent national government now controls

---

11. Bellamy, *Looking Backward*.

Hope

everything! Since all money and industry are controlled by this government, competition, selfishness, and greed are unnecessary and are replaced by nobler motives and cooperation. Because this has led to pervasive harmony, state governments and what they cost are no longer necessary, nor are political parties. All persons have their material wants satisfied, so the occurrence of crime is minimal. Therefore, there is little need of police, lawyers, and courts. Other nations have adopted the same system, so there is peace among them, and armies are a thing of the past. The great savings issuing from these wonderful improvements make general prosperity possible.

This could only become possible, says Bellamy, when people come to realize that they should no longer bemoan human depravity, but could now celebrate their divinity. We are born naturally good, in the image of God, with god-like aspirations. It is our environment that has corrupted us. We are like a rose bush planted in a swamp. Realize this, change the environment, and all things are possible. The early Gnostics could have hardly said it better.

Another analysis of the human condition is found in the works of Eckhart Tolle, a prize-winning author who represents a kind of twentieth-century version of Gnosticism.[12]

He adopted the name of the medieval mystic Meister Eckhart to reveal his views. Tolle begins with the assertion that the normal state of existence for most people is a kind of disfunction or even madness. Evil, he says, is an identification with one's physical form. Fear, greed, and a desire for power are associated with this. Let them go! You can overcome your identification with your physical form and thus become transparent to the light within you. Buddha and Jesus both taught this, according to Tolle.

The sense of "I" is at the heart of the problem. Hopefully, when things around you die (or your sense of self dies), your sense of Presence, or the "I Am," is released from its imprisonment in matter. The peace of God comes when you realize that the ultimate truth of who you are is not I am this or that, but simply, "I Am." Then you can rest in God.

12. Tolle, *New Earth*.

The American Jesus?

You are the one truth. Jesus meant this when he said, "I am the way, the truth." Buddhist and Hindus have the same idea, the indwelling god. When you become aware of your ego, you can be free of it. You deny yourself. What remains is Being, the deeper, truer "I." You can now sense that "I am that I am." Yet as Christians, we cannot help but notice that this phrase, "I Am that I am," Is the very name of God given to Moses. It is the most sacred name of God, and of God alone. It is so holy that it cannot even be pronounced by humans. This very name, according to Tolle, is exactly the one that you may apply to yourself. He means that God is at the heart of you. Only recognize it!

If you begin, in this world of suffering, says Tolle, to awaken, and see that the thinking mind cannot understand Presence, that every belief is an obstacle, then you become conscious of yourself, and understand that good and bad are ultimately illusory, then, "Your true nature emerges, which is one with the nature of God." The separation between the world and God is dissolved.

There are clearly some profound aspects of Tolle's philosophy. Yet it is also clearly at odds with some basic Christian beliefs, particularly in his teaching that we are one with God, and we must realize that "I am that I am." But any biblically based theology acknowledges what Barth called the "infinite qualitative distinction between God and man." The Eden story makes the point that our basic sin and the cause of our woes is not that we do not recognize our divinity, but precisely the opposite, that we want to play god.

Yet it is not only Tolle, but much of the American belief system that proclaims that we have god within us. Politicians, preachers, and the man on the street seem to take this for granted. It makes us feel important about ourselves, but it may be a reliance on a false self. We can feel good. This really obscures our true state and the ways to rectify it. It may be, not so much a case of lifting us up, but bringing God down to our level.

You may recall that one branch of Gnosticism in the second century did not reject the material world as their compatriots did, but rather showed their contempt for matter's lack of value by making use of it in its most extreme forms, for example in extensive eating, drinking, and sexual activity. Perhaps there is more of this type of Gnosticism in America today than is admitted, or it is simply referred to as being sophisticated and beyond the norms of the ignorant.

The question concerns the actual status of us as humans. If the Gnostics are correct, then we have God within us; we are divine, and only need to recognize this. The traditional Christian response has been that we are in no way divine, we are mortal. Live with it! We are creatures, perhaps the most exalted and beautiful of creatures, beloved by God, and living in his grace. Yet creatures still.

COLLECTIVE HOPES

America is the land of the responsible individual. And much of the appeal to faith has centered on individual decision making. The preaching of Jonathan Edwards, Billy Sunday, and Billy Graham are clear enough examples of this. Yet despite that, there has always been a social dimension to American Christianity, a dimension that is influenced by the contemporary culture, knowingly or not.

In keeping with this, America has become home to a large number of societies, or theories about society, that stress our collective nature: some recognizably Christian, some not. Some home grown. Some imported. But all pin their hopes on a better culture, a better social structure.

Bellamy was not alone. Our history is filled with actual social experiments that found the present world sinful or unjust and believed they could have a better, more virtuous life in their own communities.

We could look at the Latter Day Saints, who began in upstate New York, and moved west. They were very American in one regard, in that they believed that it was necessary to start over in faith, with a new revelation, on which they still pin their hopes. Hence the title "Latter Day." They were opposed wherever they went; likely one reason was because of their polygamy. They settled around the Great Salt Lake and have prospered in this country. One reason for this may be their very American approach to life.

The American Jesus?

They are the people of the new start. When founded, they accepted slavery and discrimination against blacks. But as America has changed, they have changed accordingly. Yet even today they are rightly admired for their virtues, such as honesty, as glowing examples of the American way. They are a countercultural group that has developed their own successful culture, which seems to have become more and more American.

Other countercultural groups include the Hutterites in the Upper Midwest. There is also the Amana Community, which lasted for many years. And many more.

The Amish, in Pennsylvania and elsewhere, are an interesting example. Escaping persecution in Europe, they eventually made it to America in the seventeenth century. They have been dedicated to avoiding any contacts with the wider culture, which they call "the English." Yet, what they are in large part preserving is not so much no culture, but the Germanic culture of the earlier period.

The Amish, despite their refusal to take part in the greater American society, may be, in a way, are an example of the dilemma we all face. What is the faith, what is the culture, that we need and want to protect and preserve?

But some other groups may even be considered bizarre in their beliefs and actions. We look at only two of them: the Shakers, and the Perfectionists at Onieda.[13]

The Shakers, established in 1792, eventually had fifty-eight communities, most of them prosperous. They were founded by "Mother Ann." She had received a revelation on which she based her religious activities. The basis of her theology was that God is both male and female. While Jesus was the expression of the male aspect of God, she, Mother Ann herself, was the expression of the female aspect.

Since in God the two aspects are one, sexual activity is an attempt to indulge in the sin of uniting the two, of "being like God." Therefore, sex is not allowed in the community. Men and women live separately, although they can eat together, in silence. There are

---

13. A good general survey of some of the American (or Americanized) religious groups in America is Nordhoff, *American Utopias*.

dances where the women dance and the men can watch, and vice versa. Of course, there is no touching.

There were many aspects to this somewhat non-indulgent community. They believed themselves to be the true church. They did not hold to most basic Christian beliefs, such as the Trinity and the atonement. They were spiritualists, believing in contact with the departed.

They prospered for a while, but eventually, since they produced no offspring, and new recruits were harder and harder to find, and sometimes did not stay, they went out of existence in the late twentieth century.

The Perfectionists, like the Shakers, were of American origin, founded by J. H. Noyes, in 1834. By the 1870s they numbered almost three hundred persons. They did believe that Jesus Christ is the Son of God. Noyes also believed that Jesus' second coming had already occurred with the destruction of Jerusalem. So, everything has changed. We are now in a new world. We are expected to live perfect lives and hold all property in common. This includes common holding of wives, which are property common to all! We may assume that this last aspect was particularly attractive to many young men. But the larger society was so repulsed by it that the practice had to be abandoned. The experiment eventually dissolved.

It is clear that religious freedom in America tends to produce a cacophony of churches, denominations, and individual eccentricities in religion, each holding out its own kind of hope in a difficult world.

But if we are to rescue any kind of hope from a world of evil and suffering, which seems determined to rob it from us, and in a culture of almost unbelievable religious variety, then we have to be clear about two things: first, what is the problem, and second, what can overcome it. There are as many diagnoses of what the disease is as there are suggested cures.

Clearly, the biblical analysis of our shattered hopes is grounded in the belief that there is something wrong, or perverse, at the heart of the human person that keeps us from being happy or good. Further, this illness results from a misplaced faith in our own selves. While recognizing the glories of the human person, the Bible insists that our hope is not to be placed in our own natural goodness or our divinity, but in God alone. From Genesis to Paul and John, the very idea of our moral purity or divinity is soundly rejected. In fact, "playing God" is at the root of our problem.

It is stated not only in Scripture, but also in some of the greatest Christian teachers, that our faith and our hope are not to be placed in our own goodness or perfection, but in God alone. Witness Irenaeus, Luther, Calvin, and many more.

The appeal to our own divine natures, or at least the hope that we are naturally good, seems endemic to much of American religious thought. Understandably, this belief necessitates jettisoning much of Christian tradition, in the name of the new, the fresh start, as new revelations in the Mormons, "Latter Day Saints," or the Shakers.

American positive thinking about our true, deep-down goodness may be attractive, be it can also be a rejection of much of the Christian tradition. It does fit well with our culture, which affirms both our native goodness and our freedom, which allows us to respond the calls of the evangelists.

This can also be seen in Bellamy, who believed that it is only a bad social organization that keeps us from realizing our true potential and happiness. Many American movements, such as the Social Gospel, have thought along the same lines. Society may be bad, they insist, but humans are good, and this goodness need only be released by appropriate social changes. Sometimes this has resulted in positive change, but often it has failed, or even brought about more suffering, such as in communist failed states.

Others have insisted that the problem is truly with the individual. It can be remedied by recognizing our true, god-like nature, they say. But Irenaeus, along with Genesis, centers our human problem precisely in our refusal to be those beautiful but merely created beings, and our desire instead to be as God. Tolle sees it in exactly the opposite way. For him it precisely in not recognizing that each of us is at heart Yahweh; that is the root of our problems.

Hope

So, in our land there is a struggle between placing our faith and our hopes in ourselves, and our own goodness and even our divinity, individually or corporately, or, like Paul and the others, admitting our basic helplessness before God, and seeking his grace.

4

Love

...and the greatest of these is love.

—1 Cor 13:13

Above all, clothe yourselves with love, which binds everything together in perfect harmony.

—Col 3:14

God is love.

—1 John 4:8

Restore in us, O God
The splendor of your love;
Renew your image in our hearts,
And all our sins remove.

—Carl P. Daw Jr.

"What the world needs now is love sweet love..." Almost everyone will agree with this thought. But there seem to be as many meanings of the term in the English language, as there are users of it. "I love my wife." "I love my country, my dog, my work."

LOVE IN THE BIBLE

In the Old Testament, God's love for his people is an ongoing theme. It is his active concern for his chosen people, his covenant love, given in the hope that they will respond with equal love. But it is a hope that is not often fulfilled. The prophet Hosea reveals the agony of a God who loves and is not loved in return. Hosea marries a prostitute, just as God has united himself with a people who are unfaithful. He takes her back again and again, just as God takes back Israel, which is playing its own kind of prostitution with other gods. Hosea expresses God's plea, "I desire steadfast love and not sacrifice..." (Hos 6:6). He predicts that the nation will be punished for its unfaithfulness, yet God's love will triumph in the end.

The Psalms are filed with joy over God's love. This is seen most clearly in Psalm 136: "O give thanks to the Lord, for he is good. For his steadfast love endures forever..." The phrase is repeated no less than twenty-eight times, so basking in his love and rejoicing in it are central to the faith of the psalmist.

We might notice two things about this divine love. First, God's love is primary. His love precedes any human response. It is God, not man, who takes the first step. Second, this love is given to a rebellious people who seldom if ever deserve it. These themes will become even more apparent in the New Testament.

The New Testament was not written in English, but in *koine*, or common, Greek. In Greek there are three basic words for love. First, there is *eros*, or sexual attraction. Interestingly, this word does not appear at all in the New Testament, either as something positive or negative. It is simply not there! The second is *philos*, or friendship, which appears occasionally.

But the third is *agape*, or the verb form, *agapao*. Together they are found more than 220 times in the New Testament, primarily in the Johannine literature and in the writings of Paul. It is interesting that it is seldom or never found outside of, or before, the New Testament. So, it can be thought of as a specifically Christian term. It is variously rendered as "good will," "self-giving," "other-regarding love," "to have reverence for," or "to take delight in." It is almost always connected with some action on the part of the one who loves, which keeps it separated from being mere sentimentality.

It is used variously to describe God's self-giving love to us, seen especially in the cross of Christ, or our own love to the Father, to Christ, and our own self-giving love to one another.

Jesus did not speak Greek, but what we have of his words are given to us in the Greek equivalent. That equivalent is usually *agapao*, or the active aspect of love, and Jesus refers to the Jewish "love God and neighbor "in its various forms. For him, this is the summary of the entire law, which frees him from any legalism, although he often connects it with justice. Love without justice is sheer sentimentality. Justice without love is merely harsh.

But Jesus expands on this theme. We are to love those who do not love us, even our enemies and those who misuse us. And we are to love God above all else, since no one can really serve two masters.

But where we encounter the bulk of references to *agape* is in the writings of Paul and John.

Agape in Paul

Agape/agapao is found in copious amounts in Paul. We know that Paul is the great man of faith in the New Testament. But he never leaves us with just that. It always leads to love and is often coupled with it. An example of this is Romans 5:5, as we have already seen. After sharing with us his persistent theme of justification by faith, he goes on to declare that because of this faith we have hope, and then proclaims that "the love of God has been poured into our hearts through the Holy Spirit that has been given us." So, faith, hope, and love are again united.

Yet there are a number of important questions surrounding this verse. One is grammatical: Is the "of" here a subjective or an objective genitive? That is, is Paul here writing of the love of God as his love to us, or of our love to him? Is God loving us, or is he enabling us to love him?

Most commentators suggest that Paul here refers to God's love to us as the primary meaning. This is in keeping with Paul's consistent theme of God's initiative in our faith and life. Just as we cannot trust him without his initiative, neither can we love him without his gift. We cannot love either God or one another as we should unless God's own love is poured into us by his Spirit. So, just as with faith, *agape* love is a gift of God, not something that we are able to conjure up in ourselves by our own goodness or efforts.

There are two important things connected to this. First, this love is associated with Christ, and what he has done for us: "I live by faith in the son of God, who loved me and gave himself for me"; "God, who is rich in mercy, out of his great love, made us alive in Christ"; "Christ loved us and gave himself for us" (Gal 2:20; Eph 2:4; 5:2).

But, as we saw in the third chapter of Romans, this love is not only associated with Christ, but also with the Holy Spirit. Paul insists that God gives his Spirit to the believers. We are temples of the Spirit. We are sanctified by this same Spirit. Paul appeals to us by our Lord Jesus Christ and the love of the Spirit, and any sharing of the Spirit. He offers his benediction, "The grace of Lord Jesus Christ, the love of God, and the communion of the Holy Spirit be with you" (2 Cor 13:13). Thus, he unites grace, Christ, God's love, and the Holy Spirit together.

But all of this leads us to our own personal behavior, especially in the loving of one another. On at least twenty-five occasions Paul makes this connection. "Love one another," he says. Love even the offender. He reminds the Ephesians, not only of their faith in Christ, but also of their love to all the saints. The essence of the Christian life is "faith working through love." (Rom 12:10; Col 5:06)

Agape in John

God's love is central to John. In both the Gospel and the First Epistle, we find the radical statement, "God is love!" (1 John 4:16) Perhaps the most quoted verse in the Bible is John 3:16, "God so loved the world that he gave his only Son, so that everyone who believes in him may not perish but may have eternal life."

The American Jesus?

But this love to us is realized in God's giving of his Son, and in the Son's self-giving. "My Father loves me," Jesus says, "because I lay down my life . . ." (John 10:17). Again and again, the books of John insist that God's, and the Son's, love is shown in sacrifice for those that are loved. There is no greater love than this, Jesus says, than to lay down one's life for one's friends (John 15:13). John goes on to affirm, as with Paul, that God takes the initiative in this love. He says that "this is love, not that we loved God, but he loved us and sent his Son." It is all grace: Christ is "full of grace and truth" (John 1:14).

Again, as with Paul, our response is to be obedient to his command. And that command is that we love one another. It is by this love that people will know that we are his disciples.

It is hard to find anywhere in the Bible where one theme stands out so strongly as does the theme of love in Paul and John. It is God who first loves us, and we in turn are to love him and keep his command to love others.

AGAPE IN THE EARLY CHURCH

It is somewhat surprising that, given the emphasis on love in Paul and John, the early church seems be so little concerned with it. There is much at this time on the contrast of the morality of the Christian life with that of the pagans. There are numerous encouragements to faithfulness, even to martyrdom. There are even attempts at displaying the rationality of the faith, as we saw in Justin, but little on God's unmerited love to us.

Yet, through most of the church's history, it could not avoid dealing with love as a central theme for any Christian, struggling to survive as a Christian in a world that sees love as either a selfish *gratification* or mere sentimentalism.

LOVE IN AUGUSTINE

> Lord, you have made us for yourself
> And our hearts are restless,
> Until they find their rest in Thee.[1]

This prayer opens his famous *Confessions*, in which the fourth- and fifth-century bishop of Hippo in North Africa traces his inner history and struggles. As he thinks through these moral struggles, he begins to reduce them to matters of love. He recalls that in his youthful years he was obsessed with love. He tells us that he could not imagine being happy unless in the arms of a woman. "I loved love itself," he says. Here we see the close connection between love and happiness that will remain with him throughout his life.

To put it more directly, he says that happiness is possessing what you love most. But you must love the right thing, or you will end in unhappiness. That "right thing" must have three qualifications to be satisfying, he says: First, the object must be truly good. For if you love it, and obtain it, but it is not good, you will be unhappy. Second, it must really be obtainable. If you do love it, and it is good, but you cannot obtain it, you will still be unhappy. Third, it must be something that cannot be taken away against your will. Just about everything can be taken from you: friends, riches, health, and even life itself. There is only one thing that can never be taken from you: God! He is good. Indeed, the ultimate good. He is obtainable, since he is always there, if only we would be looking. Also, everything else can be lost or taken away, but not God.[2]

His basic problem in his whole journey in life up to his conversion was loving the wrong things. His love of women never lived up to the promises it made. He delighted in the love he had for his best friend. But that friend died and was taken away against Augustine's will. His success, though considerable, was not satisfying. Only God could satisfy his longings. But it would take considerable time before he realized this.

1. Augustine, *Confessions* 1.1.
2. Augustine, *Exposition on the Epistle to the Romans* 4.4, 5; in *Augustine on Romans*.

The American Jesus?

Even his own considerable mental abilities, although satisfying in their own way, and adding to his self-esteem, left him lacking in self-satisfaction. In one of his early works, *The Happy Life*, he comments that the philosophers (of which he was one) were the most miserable of men. They know the goal, which is God, but because of their arrogance they cannot see that the humble Christ is the way to that goal. It is not possible for them. They cannot accept this humble Jesus, who is the only road there.

In his life as priest and then as bishop, he began to see the need for God's grace for his salvation, rather than relying on his own arrogance. The secret was to receive God's love for him in Jesus Christ. But, in our sorry state, how can we conjure up our own love of him? We cannot! As Augustine develops in his thinking, he comes more and more to cite Romans 5:5, ". . . and hope does not disappoint us, because God's love has been poured into our hearts by the Holy Spirit that has been given to us."

For Augustine, the one thing necessary for our happiness and our ultimate salvation is to love most what is best. That is, to love God above all things. The human tragedy is found precisely here, that this is the one thing that we cannot do! We love ourselves and things that please us more than we can love God.

But God's own love of himself—the mutual love of Father and Son to each other and to the Holy Spirit—has been given to us so that we may love him by his own love, which we are incapable of doing by ourselves. But that love is now ours as a gift, in the person of the Holy Spirit, which, for Augustine, equals the very love of God.[3]

In his work *On the Trinity*, Augustine resorts to numerous allegories that at least suggest the unknowable Trinity to the reader. In one of these, he uses the analogy of lover, love, beloved. The Father loves the Son, the Son loves the Father, and the Holy Spirit is that love. The very love of God is shed into our hearts that we may love him with the very love by which he loves himself. This is only an analogy, but it gives us some insight into Augustine's thinking about God's love to us and our own love to God, and how both are examples of grace.

3. Augustine, *On the Proceedings of Pelagius* 33, 34.

Love

As we saw when we looked at Augustine's idea of faith, the initiative is not ours, but God's. The beginning, the middle, and the end are from him. The same is true of our love to God. It is only by his love, which comes first, that we can love him.

We saw in the chapter on faith that for Augustine we cannot have faith without the gracious gift of God. So also with love. It is God's gift![4]

CHRISTIAN LOVE IN THE MIDDLE AGES

In the Middle Ages, as we have seen, believers struggled to understand their faith in a chaotic world. Sometimes following Augustine, sometimes unaware of his works, they tried to work out for themselves and others what this Christian love might mean in a world and a culture that seemed always to be shifting before their very eyes, a culture very much like ours. We might find it helpful to look at some of their attempts.

Francis of Assisi (d. 1226)

Perhaps the best known and most beloved of saints is Francis of Assisi. He is a kind of love incarnate. He loved the birds and the little animals. But more than that, he loved his fellow humans in the name of Christ. His goal was to be an imitator of Christ.

Several stories are told of him. In one of them, in his compassion for the poor, he took fabrics from his father's store and gave them away. His father objected. They took the matter to the local bishop, and a hearing was held in front of the cathedral. His father complained that Francis owed everything to him. Francis agreed, took off all his clothes, and handed them to his father. He then walked off, naked.

Francis insisted on absolute poverty for himself and his followers. This was not because he was legalistically bound to a literal interpretation of the Gospel. Rather, it was from a profound

---

4. Augustine, *To Simplician* 1.2.2-3.

understanding of the Christian life. He knew that attachment to possessions, and our attempts to guard and preserve them, can keep us from being open to the needs of others. Our own poverty can free us to love and serve others.

He humbly approached Pope Innocent III to request the recognition of his order. It was granted. There is a painting that well describes the best of the Middle Ages. It pictures humble Francis before one of the most powerful popes in history. Somehow, that age could contain both in some kind of harmony.

Soon, Francis's insistence on poverty was questioned by some of his followers. He insisted on its preservation, so a split ensued. Some, perhaps more practical, believed that some property was necessary. It may be that the individual could maintain poverty, but the order needed to have possessions in common. Francis did not agree.

Peter Abelard (d. 1142)

Abelard rejects any idea that the death of Christ on the cross somehow propitiated an angry God. Rather, for Abelard, by the death of Christ we see how great God's love is for us, and we in turn come to love him. There is no paying of any price to God or the devil here. The effect is entirely within us! It is subjective. Thus, this is called the subjective theory of the atonement.

Abelard's views on this and other matters led others, including Bernard of Clairvaux, to reject his version of Christ's work. But it is still popular today, especially among liberal Christians.

Bernard of Clairvaux (d. 1153)

Bernard was a member of one of the most influential of the medieval orders. And he himself was influential in large part because of his character and accomplishments. These accomplishments were immense. He founded the monastery at Clairvaux. He was called upon to encourage support for the Second Crusade. He was able to heal a papal schism.

But a major contribution of his was his theology of the stages of the Christian life in terms of the four stages of love:

At first, we love ourselves for ourselves.

The second stage is where we see that God provides for us, so we love him for what he does for us.

Then, seeing how good he is, we love him for himself.

Fourth, we come to love ourselves only for the sake of God. This is the most perfect love of God.

Thomas Aquinas (d. 1274)

Thomas, as we have already seen, is one of the towering intellects of his age or any age. He was true to the teachings of Augustine. But he saw Christianity through the eyes of the newly discovered philosophy of Aristotle, rather than Augustine's reliance on Plato. In terms of his ethics, he accepted the four cardinal virtues of Aristotle: courage, temperance, justice, and wisdom. Thomas believed that these are intended for all humans, Christian or not. But "on top" of these, for the Christian, he listed faith, which permeated and "informed," or gave proper form to, the lower, classical virtues. But faith itself is informed by hope, and all six virtues are given proper form by the highest theological virtue of love, *charitas*, which should shape our entire ethical view. This is not really like some layer cake. Rather, the higher, theological virtues permeate the lower ones. And the highest of all, Christian love, this *charitas*, must permeate the whole of a person's moral life is incomplete.

For Thomas, it is all grace. In commenting on Romans 5:5, "... the love of God is shed abroad in our hearts by the Holy spirit which is given to us," he observes that this love is infused in us by the Holy Spirit. This is not a natural ability of ours. It is given gratuitously. It exceeds the capacity of our nature. It is the love (*amor*) of the Father and the Son, and so it is in fact a communication of the supernatural to us.[5]

Love to God is the capstone of all our virtues. But it is not something we can work up in our hearts by trying harder. It is God's gift. We, of course, must have the proper disposition to receive this gift, but even that disposition exceeds our natural gifts. It, too, like faith, is the work of the Spirit.

Our weak, finite human powers cannot perfect the *charitas* that is given to us, but this comes only from God, the very love by which he loves himself! So, for Thomas, as for Paul and Augustine, we must love God, but this can occur only by an act of God himself. It is all grace: grace upon grace.

THE REFORMATION

Luther shows himself to be in the mainstream of thinking about Christian love in his commentary on the central passage of Romans 5:1-5. After dwelling on Paul's insistence on the necessity of faith, he goes on to apply the same insistence to our love to this God. He says that ". . . this sublime power which is in us is not from ourselves, but must be sought from God. And this takes place through the Holy Spirit; it is not acquired by moral effort and practice . . . Who has been given to us, that is, whom we do not deserve . . ."[6]

But other than here and a few other places, there is very little in Luther directly about our love to God. This may possibly be explained by the fact that the theology of much of the church at this time was at least semi-Pelagian, often stressing our own spiritual accomplishments, our own love, rather than the grace of God. The important battle, as he saw it, was to vigorously oppose this tendency to slip into a faith in our own effort or love, rather than relying on God alone.

---

5. Aquinas, *Summa Contra Gentiles*, first part of the second part, as cited in Pegis, "Introduction," xi–xiv.

6. Luther, *Lectures on Romans*, 294.

Love

Yet what amounts to love of neighbor is certainly there, especially in Luther's insistence, in *On Christian Liberty*, that by faith in Christ we are freed to spend our lives in service to others.

The following Lutherans were understandably obsessed with establishing *sola fide*, or "faith alone," as over against the legalisms of their day. But their insistence on this tended to lead to a lack of stress on the Holy Spirit and God's love to us and our responsive love to God.

This lack, for its part, also led to a reaction in many Protestants, who felt that an essential part of their faith was being neglected: the love to God and neighbor that only God himself can bring. One of these was the Moravian revival under Count Zinzendorf.

ZINZENDORF AND THE MORAVIANS

In the post-Reformation period, while both Protestantism and Catholicism were casting stones against each other and therefore becoming more and more rigid in their presentations, many believers were seeking refuge in a more humane faith. This was evident in the Pietist movement in Germany and elsewhere. It stressed a more practical, experiential faith. This movement had its beginning in Germany and then beyond. Count Zinzendorf of Saxony (d. 1760) was clearly affected by the Moravians. He always held a deep passionate devotion to Christ, emphasizing a religion of the heart.

He was count of Saxony and gave refuge to a group of believers from Moravia. These "Moravians" were the followers of Jon Huss, who had been burned at the stake by the Council of Constance, and they still faced persecution. Zinzendorf not only allowed them to stay, in a settlement called Herrnhut, but actually became their bishop.

Zinzendorf and the Moravians influenced each other. Their calling was not only to bask in God's love, but also to share the good news to all whom they could inform. Like other Pietists, they went everywhere. They especially went from Herrnhut over much of Europe with their message. They did not attempt to take over the

The American Jesus?

state churches, but to enliven them. While they were often resisted by these established churches, they did have a profound effect in these areas, and Pietism became an important influence in places such as Sweden and Norway. Many of the settlers in America from Europe were Pietists and have had, in their turn, a profound influence on the shape of religion in America.

JOHN WESLEY AND THE METHODISTS IN AMERICA

The American colonies were a kind of hodgepodge of religions. Puritanism dominated in New England; the Anglican Church in the remainder of the colonies, with the exception of Rhode Island and Pennsylvania, which had their own forms of religious expression. But there were all kinds of differing religious expressions allowed, since America needed settlers of all stripes.

The English crown founded a settlement in Georgia, partly as a buffer between their colonies and the Spanish in Florida. Many of its new residents were those released from debtor's prison on the condition that they would settle there.

James Oglethorpe was tapped to be Georgia's governor. He intended to organize this colony on Christian principles. No large property holdings were permitted; alcohol was not allowed, nor was slavery. Yet in just a few years all of these restrictions were abandoned.

One of the Anglican clergymen to serve there was John Wesley. He and his brother Charles and George Whitefield had been fellow students at Oxford. As sincere and pious students, they studied and prayed together, being given the nickname "Methodists" by the other students.

As John sailed to America to serve as pastor at Savannah, the ship was in grave danger in a storm. The rather stiff Wesley was impressed by a group of Moravians, who seemed calm even in the storm.

In Savannah, John was somewhat less than successful. He left discouraged. But, back in England, involved again with a group of

Moravians, he attended one of their meetings at Aldersgate. There, while they were reading from Luther's *Commentary on Romans*, he felt a "strange warming of the heart."

From now on, Wesley would be a different, inspired man, and through him and his associates Methodism became a dynamic religious and social force in England: a Pietist force of considerable power. Such social reforms as the end of slavery in England are attributed to their work.

The three men responsible for this were an amazing trio: John was the great organizer; his brother Charles, the wonderful hymn writer; and Whitefield was a great preacher, of whom it was said that he could charm the birds out of the trees.

But the greatest influence of Methodism was in America. There was already a religious revival stirring in the colonies: among the Puritans in New England with Jonathan Edwards, and also in New Jersey. But the Methodists seemed best at it.

For one thing, they were dedicated. Some have mused that while the Lutherans would only go into the American frontier by stagecoach, and the Anglicans waited for Pullmans, the Methodist evangelists would ride into the wilderness on horseback, appealing to the unchurched, who were often far from the influence of any organized religion.

Methodism grew like wildfire, and quickly became one of the most important and influential religious movements in American society. There was a myriad of camp meetings, where, sometimes for days on end, dedicated and emotional preachers would appeal to the unchurched or semichurched crowds, inviting them to turn from their sins and come to the Lord.

By the year 1800, Methodism had grown to be one of the dominant denominations in the USA. Its success can be attributed in part to the dedication and enthusiasm of its clergy. But it can also be seen as successful because it appealed to something basic in American culture and in the American psyche.

For one thing, it appealed to the American belief in free will. A basic mark of Americanism is, and has always been, an insistence on personal responsibility. We each have the liberty, and

The American Jesus?

indeed the responsibility, to make our own decisions. The constant call of the ever—moving frontier bids us to have the courage to decide for ourselves and to suffer the consequences (good or bad) of our choices.

Wesley's theology was a perfect fit for the American insistence on the need to make our own decisions, in religion as in the rest of life. He truly detested the whole notion of predestination, which sees us as helpless unless God himself acts within us. Thus, he completely rejected the understanding of Christianity held by Augustine, Thomas, Luther, and Calvin. For them it was a necessary corollary of grace. It says that we cannot love God unless he first intervenes in our disoriented souls. For Wesley, this was a way of avoiding the need for that human decision by which we turn to God.

In fact, as we have seen earlier, Wesley wrote a tract entitled, *Predestination, Calmly Considered*. It was actually not very calm at all. Wesley was clearly upset by the very thought that we are not able to make that decision which is so very necessary for our salvation. How could evangelists appeal to the hordes of penitent sinners if they are not able to respond? But it is interesting that Whitefield, probably the best preacher of them all, did believe in predestination.

Methodism has had a great influence on the American psyche and religion. This is certainly true in part because it appeals to our psyche in the first place. So the question must be raised whether Methodism is a valid plea for the Christianization of America or the cultural Americanization of Christianity.

SCHLEIERMACHER: SOPHISTICATED PIETISM

It is difficult to find a person who better illustrates the tension between faith and culture, and the place of feeling for the Christian, than in the life and work of Friedrich Schleiermacher (d. 1834). He was highly educated and traveled within the sophisticated intellectual circles of his time. He was familiar with the writings of Kant and others. Yet he was a devout believer, having experienced part

Love

of his education at Halle, a Moravian university. So, like Wesley, he was influenced by them to some extent, with their emphasis on a warm-hearted religion.

In 1799 he published *On Religion: Speeches to Its Cultured Despisers*.[7] Clearly, he himself was a sophisticate; perhaps he was describing his own struggles. Many of these "despisers" saw religion as either cold intellectualism, stressing correct doctrine, or as constricting moralism. "No!" he said. It is neither. It is a matter of feeling: the feeling and intuition of the universe, the sense of the infinite in the finite. Later he would describe it merely as "feeling," the immediate feeling of God. A feeling of absolute dependence.

Jesus is central to this experience. Schleiermacher rejected the classical theological expression of Jesus' person, but insisted that Jesus' God-consciousness was so central to his existence that it was a veritable existence of God within him. In this sense, for him, Jesus can be called both human and divine.

Although Schleiermacher was harshly criticized by Karl Barth and others as essentially basing Christianity on his culture, his influence was, and to some extent still is, immense. For many, his theology allows them to maintain a Christian faith, but in the context of the modern world. This was already true in his lifetime. It was reported that over twenty thousand persons were in his funeral procession.

We saw in the chapter on faith that the great traditions of Christianity insisted that even this faith is not possible without its being a gift of God, and that seems troublesome to the American "can do" spirit. So also, with the kind of love in the Bible, *agape* or *charis*, it is a gift from God himself, something we cannot muster up on our own. The question is whether, and in what ways, this can be somehow made to be consistent with that same American spirit.

...for at the heart of our universe is a higher reality—God and his kingdom of love—to which we must be conformed.
—MARTIN LUTHER KING JR., *STRENGTH TO LOVE*

7. Schleiermacher, *On Religion*.

Afterthoughts/Conclusions

Do not be conformed to this world, but be transformed by the renewing of your minds...

—Rom 12:2

As we look at the present scene, at left and right, liberal Christians and conservative Christians, and how they consider themselves and the other believers, it would appear that *the* Christian virtue is arrogance or self-righteousness. This is, to some extent, what is being practiced.

We find there is a host of understandings of what Christianity is, and what it is all about. Some groups will stress one aspect of the faith, while others emphasize others.

Liberals seize on certain aspects, conservatives on different ones. Various biblical passages may be important to some, others to others.

This kaleidoscope of expressions of what purports to be "one faith" seems particularly evident in America, where freedom of religion has blossomed into a myriad of churches and denominations. We seem to be like children at a candy store, choosing whatever suits our fancy, and whatever expresses best what we already believe. Our neighbor, of course, has every right to choose something else. Even though it is messy, American Christianity has been one of the most successful and exciting expressions of the Christian faith(s) at any time and in any place.

Afterthoughts/Conclusions

Yet we are left with a belief that just about anything can be called Christianity, or perhaps there is no real Christianity at all. Further, a host of differing expressions of the church proclaim that their way is what God himself would want, and perhaps what God insists that we follow.

Back in the 1950s, a person could purchase some vinyl (yes vinyl!) recordings with titles such as *Jazz for People Who Don't Like Jazz* or *Classical Music for People Who Don't Like Classical Music*. These records would select recordings for you that you might possibly like out of the whole collection of music of a type.

It seems that today, in Christianity in America, both for individuals and whole denominations, we tend to select whatever seems reasonable to us, or perhaps only pleases us, out of the entire catalog of teachings and practices that have been handed down to us.

It has been the position of this book that there is in fact a valid expression of what the Christian faith is, and it is well expressed in Paul's expression, "Faith, hope and love. And the greatest of these is love." Within the Scriptures and in the works of a great number of some of the greatest of Christian thinkers throughout church history, it has been seen to best express what Christianity is all about. It is also true that even in their vast variety of beliefs and practices, as different as they may be, the greatest thinkers have always insisted that all of these variations rely upon and are permeated with one central theme, the grace of God: his free, loving, undeserved gift of his acceptance of us, despite our shortcomings, and even our own resistance to that gift. We have seen this free grace as proclaimed time and time again to be central to the faith, in Paul, Augustine, Thomas, Luther, and Calvin, as different as they may be from each other in the particulars of the faith. We thus feel justified in making this formula the test of what is truly Christian, and what may be questionable.

But there is another side to this free gift of grace. That is, the satisfaction of our desperate need for the forgiveness and healing that are contained in it. All of these historical witnesses insist that we must recognize this need, despite our human tendency to deny our sinful orientation, or to try to solve it on our own.

The American Jesus?

We have also looked at the culture in which American Christianity has taken root and grown into a powerful movement, largely at home in this culture, and perhaps, to some extent, an expression of it. Perhaps it is too much at home within some of the most important of these expressions of this American culture, often taken for granted as simply true and good, which are: optimism, pluralism, relativism, secularism, and pragmatism. The important question here is whether, and to what extent, each of these marks of American culture can be expressions of, or are opposed to, this basic Christianity. Or perhaps they simply exist along side it.

As we look again at these five marks of the American belief system, we will in each case raise questions about how much each of them is in sync with the basic tenets of Christianity, and to what extent each is in tension with it.

AMERICAN OPTIMISM

A basic optimism about the human person and its potential for good is endemic to those involved in the American experience. Most immigrants throughout our history have come here because they had hope of a better life and believed that they could find it here.

This was true from the beginning. An open continent was there with the promise of a new start. Even the dour Puritans ended up, to some extent, agreeing with the positive feelings of the Unitarians, who detested the negative implications of original sin, which, they were convinced, stymied personal freedom and creativity. Certainly, the success of the positive thinking of a Peale, a Schuller, and an Osteen suggests that they are tapping into some important aspect of the American psyche.

Not only was the positive thinking about individual hopes and dreams present, but there was also similar thinking about the possibilities of a properly constructed society. Witness Jefferson and his love of the ideals of the French Revolution, despite the chaos and cruelties of that social movement. The hope here was that the proper social organization would bring out the natural

Afterthoughts/Conclusions

goodness of all, and lead to a better world. The novel *Looking Backward* expresses the belief of many Americans that a new social order will bring out the best in us and lead to a better life for all. Many of the American social experiments, especially in the nineteenth century, point to a hope for a better, happier, and more pious life for all.

As Christians, we are all, in some respects, optimists. We know that God will, by his grace, triumph in our lives and hopefully in our societies. Yet we should also be aware that some forms of these human hopes are based on beliefs that run counter to much of the teaching of the faith. In fact, despite the sincere hopes that they entail, many of them have proved disastrous to the very goals that they pretend to realize.

These hopes, which keep popping up through history, have been opposed as anti-Christian by some of the giants of the faith. Paul insisted that we are saved by faith, not in ourselves and in our accomplishments, but in the one who came to us in Jesus Christ. Augustine warred with the Pelagians, who proclaimed that we are perfectly capable by our own powers to live a perfect life. Thomas, Luther, and Calvin opposed the semi-Pelagians, who saw the Christian life as one where we can, at least in part, earn our salvation.

Irenaeus countered the Gnostics, who proclaimed that we are of one nature with God and only need to realize this oneness to gain our salvation. Today, Tolle and others happily proclaim that we are already one with God. Only realize it!

There is certainly an optimism, a positive thinking, in Christianity as well. But it needs to be tempered by a realization that there are real negative forces within society, and even, perhaps especially, within ourselves, in our own hearts and minds. Evil is real, and it must be taken seriously! Nowhere do these forces bare their teeth more obviously than in the cross of Jesus, where individual and corporate sin crucify the innocent one. But also, nowhere is the victory of God for human kind more clearly seen than in this same cross, and in the resurrection of that same crucified one. As much as we strive to find good solutions to our woes,

The American Jesus?

the ultimate victory for us and for our world relies on the One who created us as good.

PLURALISM

The U.S. military has traditionally allowed Protestant, Catholic, and Jewish chaplains in the armed services. Now they have also added Muslim and even Wicken chaplains! It seems they really mean it when they say they believe in religious pluralism. And this is clearly American.

As we have seen, the American motto could be "Go along to get along." This may be especially true in regard to religion. The idea seems to be that if we accept each other's religious differences, then we can have a peaceful, stable society. Not only do we accept a variety of religious expressions, but we also have accepted a vast number of differing social experiments in the name of religious freedom.

Since religious beliefs are usually so closely tied to particular cultures, the question still needs to be asked, in a society where so many religions are being practiced, is there any basis of social unity? Perhaps the very pluralism that we can boast unites us can be the same force that eventually tears us apart.

We have also become more and more open to differing moral lifestyles. This is particularly evident in sexuality, where homosexual, lesbian, unmarried cohabitation, and all kinds of other social behaviors are practiced and approved by the general culture. It is when anyone opposes these that they meet with social disapproval, which disapproval may itself be its own kind of bigotry.

Is religious pluralism a freedom from this bigotry? If religion is seen, not as some set of childish myths, but as one's most basic beliefs and ethical imperatives, then is pluralism not its own religion, which is just as demanding of obedience as any other? Perhaps it is in this country, which boasts of its openness, that we tend to be closed to anyone who opposes this pluralism.

When we look at the early Roman Empire, we see a society that was quite open to religious diversity. Gods from all over were

Afterthoughts/Conclusions

included in their pantheons. Yet there was one group that did not fit: the Jews, with their fierce monotheism! The earlier wars of the Maccabees, and later Roman attacks on Jewish rebels, are stern reminders of the limits of Roman tolerance.

The early Christians, too, found that Roman tolerance extended only so far. The pleas that they were good citizens and honored the emperor fell on deaf ears, since they were different and were seen as unpatriotic. And their difference centered on their insistence that they worship only one God. The vaunted Roman tolerance could not tolerate this, and so they were ostracized, and, of course, often killed by the same intolerant Romans who accused them of intolerance.

Today, many Christian believers have endured the condescending looks of elitists, who "tolerate" their ignorance. We may now already be in the period of what David Gelertner called "the world's fourth great religion." It is not Christianity, or Judaism, or Islam. It may be the one religion that trumps them all: Americanism![1]

PRAGMATISM

It is no secret that all of us seek happiness or fulfillment. The only questions are what we conceive happiness to be, and how we are to achieve it. These questions apply whether we are thinking only of our individual happiness or of a more social, corporate fulfillment. We might further ask to what extent our culture has itself colored our understanding of just what happiness is, and whether this is consistent with any specific Christian belief about human fulfillment.

Americans are a practical people, and it seems appropriate that the only philosophy of life that we have produced is pragmatism, the belief that the best test of any idea or practice is whether it "works," i.e., whether it has positive results for human life and happiness. This philosophy is so much a part of the American psyche,

---

1. Gelernter, *Americanism*.

and has led to so much success, that we hardly ever stop to think that that we are practicing it. The truth of it seems obvious to us.

But two issues remain outstanding: First and most important is the question of what "works" means. That is, do we have any understanding or agreement on the optimum goal of human existence? Second, if the goal is agreed upon, is there any consensus on the best way to get there?

For the most part, Americans seem content with realizing what is usually called "the good life." It often consists of basic health, reasonable prosperity, friends and family, safety, some measure of success, and the like. It is difficult to disagree with this understanding of what human happiness involves. Yet we still must ask what each of these ingredients entails and how they are best achieved. From a philosophical standpoint, it is necessary to ask the question of how and in what way each of these fulfills our quest for fulfillment. Even more important, it is necessary to ask what human fulfillment means, and why it seems so often far from our grasp.

When we are introduced to a game that is new to us, we always need to ask what "winning" means in that particular game. So it is with life. Unfortunately, much of our present pragmatism replies that we simply do not know that goal, but we will find it out as we go along. Perhaps we are in the situation expressed by the poet: "where ignorant armies clash by night!"

Pragmatism is always helpful in guiding us in the immediate situation but does us little good in the long run unless a greater goal, a greater calling, draws us on. Pragmatism is not so much wrong as it is incomplete. It is precisely here that the Christian faith offers us guidance. It reminds us that there is an ultimate goal that transcends, but also permeates, all of our intermediate successes or failures. That ultimate is our fulfillment at our best, made possible by faith in God and trust in his grace.

Remember that Augustine, that great teacher of grace, put it this way in his *Confessions*: "Lord, you have made us for yourself, and our hearts are restless until they find their rest in thee." He also said that the philosophers are the unhappiest of men because they

Afterthoughts/Conclusions

know the goal, but do not know the way, the humble Jesus. Perhaps today he would say that the pragmatists are in the opposite position: they think they have found the way, but do not know the goal.

It is also clear that Augustine applies this thinking to society as well. For him, the "City of God" lives within human culture, the "City of Man." But that City of God sees the ultimate goal. This places Augustine, and much of Christian thinking, in clear opposition to Cox's "Secular City," since Cox rejoices in a culture freed from religious considerations.

We all desire a good life in a good society. The struggle through the ages between Christians and secularists has been about both the goal and the way. It still is.

RELATIVISM

Relativism is the belief that all truths are relative to your viewpoint: who you are, where you are, and what attitudes you bring to the observation, either your own or that of your culture. Of course, most relativists are pretty absolute about their relativism.

This philosophy, although it goes back to some of the ancient Greeks, was given a boost in the modern popular mind by Einstein's theory of relativity. Here, Einstein insisted, such things as space and time are relative to the observer. There was, however, one thing that remained absolute, that is, the speed of light. He objected strenuously to those, like Emanuel Kant, who believed that such concepts as space and time are only the way we see things, not necessarily the way they really are. So even for him there are some things that are not merely "relative."

This theory was impressive, even for the scientifically unlettered. Part of this stemmed from the situation of the modern person. For a long time, historicism had taught us that our understanding of what is true is determined in important ways by our situation in the historical/cultural matrix. But it has become even more important for many people because of our present situation, where they personally experience how differing cultural and personal views clash, or sometimes agree, when meeting each other. This could, and sometimes has, led to a very painful social chaos. The solution has seemed obvious: no views, perhaps even my own, including religious beliefs, are absolute, but only relative to something.

It is interesting, though, that many scientists will insist that Einstein's theories of relativity are not only relatively true, but absolutely so!

In the expressions of it, relativism seems closely allied with pluralism. Both try to deal with the nagging issues of whether there is such a thing as truth, what that truth may be, how we can ever know it, and how we can ever agree upon what it may be.

It is in this sense that Americans are more prone to this relativism as a way of surviving in a hodgepodge of ideas and beliefs. It can also have a positive side, since it can strip away much of the arrogance of those who ridicule Christians for their childish beliefs without realizing the lack of basis of their own cherished ideas.

Moral values, in particular, are even more elusive than scientific ones, for non-believers as well as believers, and usually more troublesome to the human spirit. We are inundated with proclamations from on high about what is right and what is wrong and with what we are to do. But a truly pluralistic ethic is hard to maintain, especially when we are faced with real decisions in a real world, decisions that have to be made now! The fly must alight somewhere. No wonder we find ourselves confused and often unable to function in a complex and demanding world. From where will we get the guidance that we crave?

At this point postmodernism enters the arena, questioning whether there is any basis for these beliefs and values. It asks if there is any foundation for many of the things we tend to take for granted. While for some this can lead to a kind of nihilism, for others it leaves the door open for faith, which is now seen as just as necessary in the marketplace of beliefs as are the so-called hard truths in other areas.

Perhaps T. S. Elliot was right concerning a people who have lost a firm basis for their lives and beliefs:

> Lost in a haunted wood
> Children afraid of the Night,
> Who have never been happy, or Good.

Afterthoughts/Conclusions

SECULARISM

Our journey through history, as limited and selective as it has been, reveals a continuing alliance, but also a tension, between Christianity and culture, sometimes between church and state. Rome persecuted Christians. Christians persecuted heretics. Medieval popes were able at times to protect believers, but often gave way to their own ambitions. The reformers themselves became persecutors. Through it all, believers, who were often caught up in social and political squabbles, tried to make sense of the ways in which their faith and their culture could relate to each other. America, with its First Amendment, has often stumbled forward in apparently successful ways of dealing with this puzzle.

This great experiment in democracy, the United States, is one of the most amazing chapters in human history. A wilderness has been cleared, hordes of immigrants integrated, and unheard-of prosperity achieved. Added to this, a mind-boggling variety of religious expressions have found a home here, most of them claiming some connection to historic Christianity. The United States has clearly been one of the great success stories in history, in religion as well as in social, scientific, and economic achievement.

But this religious pluralism has a clear downside as well. While all faiths are affirmed, none can be held as the really true one. This is seldom what religious believers will accept, no matter what their particular set of beliefs.

The great American achievement in religion has been the separation of church and state: no manger scenes on public lands, no prayers that are addressed to any particular god, and no Christmas carols in school. This has taken place at the same time that the state has come to control more and more of public life, so faith becomes less and less important, except in the corners of one's private life.

But it may be that all of these troublesome variations are really children of the one parent: secularism! Perhaps the non-establishment clause is really establishing this secularism as the one ultimate belief before which all others must bow. Its cousin, multiculturalism, becomes the one true religion, which can suck the life out of

The American Jesus?

all the others, rather than really affirming any of them. And woe to anyone who questions secularism and its partner, multiculturalism. It would be un-American! Of course, this approach to the matter is much more preferable to most of us than the state as the determiner of what we are to believe, as best illustrated by the excesses of the French Revolution or the cruelties of Stalinism.

But now the difficult question also arises, whether this aspect of American religion is, at its heart, atheistic! It was that brilliant atheist Nietzsche who perceived that the modern secularist state finds that it has no need of Christianity, or perhaps of any religion whatever. Since all religions are equally acceptable, none of them is really true or even important.

Since Nietzsche clearly saw the root of atheism in the modern world, despite its protestations to the contrary, he also saw the tragedy of it: that our world has lost its center, its sun that holds the planets together, and, as he said, there is no up or down left. For him this was a terrible tragedy, but he felt he must have the courage to see it.

The simple question is still with us: We strive to be both good Americans and good Christians. Are they the same thing? Are they completely opposed? Or, do they overlap in important ways? And if so, how and where? We have seen that we are not alone is this battle, but a great host of witnesses has gone before us and can give us some guidance and encouragement as we struggle with some of the same problems, but in ever new dress.

As we face attacks upon the Christian faith from within and without, and the confusion with which most of us endure them, and as we try to relate that faith to our ever changing and very demanding world, we may take some comfort when we realize that we have seen this movie before. Our problems, although new in some respects, have befuddled and challenged believers, in one form or another, for centuries. And Christians have met them with various degrees of success. So, as members of the enduring church, and also as members of this "brave new world," as citizens of that great social experiment the United States, we can also cling to our marching orders of Faith, Hope, and Love.

Bibliography

Aulen, Gustaf. *Christus Victor*. Translated by A. G. Hebert. Eugene, OR: Wipf and Stock, 2003.

Augustine. *Augustine on Romans: Propositions from the Epistle to the Romans: Unfinished Commentary on the Epistle to the Romans*. Translated and edited by Paula Fredriksen Landes. Early Christian Literature Series 6, Texts and Translations 23. Chico, CA: Scholars, 1982.

———. *Confessions*. In vol. 1 of *The Nicene and Post Nicene Fathers*, series 1, edited by Philip Shaff. Reprint, Peabody, MA: Hendrickson, 1994.

———. *The Enchiridion on Faith, Hope and Love*. Edited by Harry Paolucci. Chicago: Regnery, 1961.

———. *On Nature and Grace*. In vol. 5 of The Nicene and Post Nicene Fathers, series 1, edited by Philip Shaff. Reprint, Peabody, MA: Hendrickson, 1994.

———. *On the Proceedings of Pelagius*. In vol. 5 of The Nicene and Post Nicene Fathers, series 1, edited by Philip Shaff. Reprint, Peabody, MA: Hendrickson, 1994.

———. *On the Spirit and the Letter*. In vol. 5 of *The Nicene and Post Nicene Fathers*, series 1, edited by Philip Shaff. Reprint, Peabody, MA: Hendrickson, 1994.

———. *To Simplician*. In vol. 1 of *The Nicene and Post Nicene Fathers*, series 1, edited by Philip Shaff. Reprint, Peabody, MA: Hendrickson, 1994.

Bainton, Roland. *Here I Stand: A Life of Martin Luther*. New York: Metor, 1950.

Baker, Joseph O., and Buster G. Smith. *American Secularism: Cultural Contours of Non-Religious Belief Systems*. New York: New York University Press, 2015.

Becker, Carl. *The Heavenly City of the Eighteenth-Century Philosophers*. New Haven, CT: Yale University Press, 1965.

Bellamy, Edward. *Looking Backward 2000–1887*. Boston: Houghton, Mifflin, 1890.

Brown, Peter. *Augustine of Hippo: A Biography*. Berkeley: University of California Press, 1967.Carlson, D. A. *Christ and Culture Revisited*. Grand Rapids: Eerdmans, 2008.

Channing, William Ellery. "Unitarian Christianity." Sermon delivered in Baltimore, 1819.

Cox, Harvey. *The Secular City: A Celebration of Its Liberation and an Invitation to Its Discipline*. New York: Macmillan, 1965.

Bibliography

Descartes, René. *Descartes: Philosophical Writings*. Translated by Norman Kemp Smith. New York: Modern Library, 1958.

Gelernter, David. *Americanism: The Fourth Great Western Religion*. New York: Doubleday, 2007.

Herberg, Will. *Protestant, Catholic, Jew: An Essay in American Religious Sociology*. Chicago: University of Chicago Press, 1960.

Irenaeus. *Against Heresies*. In vol. 1 of *The Ante-Nicene Fathers*, edited by Alexander Roberts and James Donaldson. Reprint, Peabody, MA: Hendrickson, 1994.

Kant, Immanuel. *Critique of Pure Reason*. Translated by Norman Kemp Smith. New York: St. Martin's, 1908.

Kaufmann, Walter. *Nietzche: Philosopher, Psychologist, Antichrist*. 4th ed. Princeton, NJ: Princeton University Press, 1974.

Leinhard, Marc. *Luther: Witness to Jesus Christ*. Translated by Edwin H. Robertson. Minneapolis: Augsburg, 1982.

Luther, Martin. *Concerning Christian Liberty*. Produced by Elizabeth T. Knuth and David Widger. Project Gutenberg, 2013. https://www.gutenberg.org/ebooks/1911 .

———. *Lectures on Romans*. In vol. 25 of *Luther's Works*, edited by H. C. Oswald. St. Louis, MO: Concordia, 1972.

———. *Selected Writings of Martin Luther*. Editd by Theodore G. Tappert. 4 vols. Minneapolis: Fortress, 2007.

Lutheran Book of Worship. Minneapolis: Augsburg, 1978.

Moore, Russell D. *Onward: Engaging the Culture Without Losing the Gospel*. Nashville: B&H, 2015.

Niebuhr, H. Richard. *Christ and Culture*. New York: Harper, 1951.

Nordhoff, Charles. *American Utopias*. Stockbridge, MA: Berkshire House, 1993.

Osteen, Joel. *You Best Life Now: 7 Steps to Living at Your Full Potential*. New York: Faith Words, 2007.

Pegis, Anton C. "Introduction." In *Basic Writings of Saint Thomas Aquinas*, edited by Anton C. Pegis. New York: Random House, 1944.

Pelagius. *The Letters of Pelagius: Celtic Soul Friend*. Edited by Robert Van de Weyer. Evesham: Arthur James, 1995.

Penner, Myron B., editor. *Christianity and the Postmodern Turn: Six Views*. Grand Rapids: Brazos, 2005.

Rousseau, Jean-Jacques. *The Social Contract*. Translated by Maurice Cranston. New York: Penguin, 1993.

Rudolph, Kurt. *Gnosis: The Nature and History of Gnosticism*. Translated by Robert Wilson. San Francisco: HarperSanFrancisco, 1987.

Schleiermacher, Friedrich. *On Religion: Speeches to Its Cultural Despisers*. Translated by John Oman. New York: Harper, 1958.

Tolle, Eckhart. *A New Earth: Awakening to Your Life's Purpose*. New York: Penguin, 2005.

Walker, Williston. *A History of the Christian Church*. 3rd ed. New York: Scribner, 1970.

www.ingramcontent.com/pod-product-compliance
Lightning Source LLC
Chambersburg PA
CBHW070930160426
43193CB00011B/1637